MW00564280

THE
CAMERA'S COAST

HISTORIC IMAGES
OF SHIP AND SHORE *in New England*

W. H. BUNTING

Introduction by JOHN R. STILGOE

HISTORIC NEW ENGLAND

Boston 2006

DONOR ACKNOWLEDGMENTS

We extend our sincere appreciation to
the following donors:

PATRONS
Harold J. Carroll
Mr. and Mrs. Richard Cheek
Anonymous Donor

SPONSORS
The Lunder Foundation
Carl R. Nold
Jean S. and Frederic A. Sharf

Additional support from
Lorna Condon, Drs. John and Françoise Little,
Susanna Crampton, Mr. and Mrs. Daniel M. Kimball,
Denise A. Trapani, Rosamond B. Vaule

Historic New England
141 Cambridge Street
Boston, Massachusetts 02114
www.HistoricNewEngland.org

Distributed by Tilbury House, Publishers
2 Mechanic Street
Gardiner, Maine 04345
www.tilburyhouse.com
800-582-1899

Copyright 2006 by Historic New England
All rights reserved. No part of this publication may be reproduced
or transmitted in any form or by any means, electronic or mechanical,
including photocopy, recording, or any information storage or
retrieval system, without permission in writing from the publisher.

First Edition 2006

Library of Congress Cataloging-in-Publication Data
Bunting, William Henry, 1945–
The camera's coast : historic images of ship and shore in New England
/ W.H. Bunting ; introduction by John R. Stilgoe.—1st ed.
    p. cm.
Historic photographs from an exhibition entitled The camera's coast
drawn from the library and archives of Historic New England.
    ISBN-10: 0-88448-287-1 (hardcover : alk. paper)
    ISBN-13: 978-0-88448-287-1 (hardcover : alk. paper)
1. Atlantic Coast (New England)—History—Pictorial works—Exhibitions.
2. Atlantic Coast (New England)—Social life and customs—Pictorial works—
Exhibitions. 3. New England—History, Local—Pictorial works—Exhibitions.
4. Seashore—Atlantic Coast (New England)—History—Pictorial works—
Exhibitions. 5. Historic buildings—Atlantic Coast (New England)—Pictorial
works—Exhibitions. 6. Ships—Atlantic Coast (New England)—History—
Pictorial works—Exhibitions. 7. Fishing—Atlantic Coast (New England)—
History—Pictorial works—Exhibitions. 8. Fishers—Atlantic Coast (New
England)—History—Pictorial works—Exhibitions. 9. Fisheries—Atlantic
Coast (New England)—History—Pictorial works—Exhibitions. I. Historic
New England (Organization) II. Title.
    F12.A74B86 2006
    974—dc22   2006018954

FRONT COVER: *Independence,* 1884, by Nathaniel L. Stebbins (top);
Postcard of Paragon Park, Nantasket Beach, Massachusetts, c. 1906 (bottom).
BACK COVER: "Picture Puzzle" game box, c. 1889, manufactured by
McLoughlin Bros., New York, private collection.
INSIDE FRONT FLAP AND COVER: Negative image of the *Independ-
ence,* 1884, by Nathaniel L. Stebbins.
INSIDE BACK FLAP AND COVER: Negative image of the *City of Bangor,*
1906, by Nathaniel L. Stebbins.
FRONT FLAP, PAGE ONE, AND BACK FLAP: Postcard of the steamer
Uncatena, Oak Bluffs, Massachusetts.
FRONTISPIECE: Marine view from Oak Bluffs, Martha's Vineyard,
Massachusetts, c. 1870, photographer unknown.

Book and cover design by Julia Sedykh Design
Illustrations edited by W. H. Bunting, Richard Cheek, and Lorna Condon
Copyedited by Nancy Curtis
Digital imaging by W. E. Andrews, an RR Donnelley Company, Bedford,
    Massachusetts
Printed and bound in China by C&C Offset Printing Co., Ltd.

FOREWORD

AMID THE TANGIBLE treasures assembled over ninety-six years by Historic New England are buildings, landscapes, artifacts, documents, and photographs representing four centuries of New England life. We value these things today especially for the stories they tell of lives and times now gone by.

Research tells us that people think of history as "anything before me," so the present quickly becomes the past, and the past is quickly forgotten unless reminders are preserved. Thanks to a proposal developed by two long-time friends, Richard Cheek and Earle G. Shettleworth, Jr., Historic New England embarks with this volume on a new series of publications that will enable us to share our rich resources with those who want to know more about New England's past.

In his selection of photographs and eloquent text, author Bill Bunting brings to bear his extraordinary knowledge of coastal New England history and of the maritime trades, recounting the sometimes humorous, sometimes tragic, but always fascinating stories the images have to tell. In his introductory essay, distinguished Harvard University historian John R. Stilgoe speaks of the power those images have to evoke another era, to permanently fix otherwise fleeting scenes, to convey actions or stillness, and to engage the viewer in contemplation and with emotion.

The trustees and staff of Historic New England are committed to making our collections fully accessible to large and diverse audiences. We are grateful to generations of donors who contributed the one million documents, photographs, architectural records, items of ephemera, and manuscripts that make up these collections. In this volume, we are delighted to make some of them available for all to enjoy. This book is the first in a series that will feature the collections in new ways, organized in themes that will appeal to both the specialist and the casual reader. Historic New England thanks all who contributed to this project.

Carl R. Nold
President and C E O
HISTORIC NEW ENGLAND
Boston, Massachusetts

EDITOR'S NOTE

WITH SEVENTY-FIVE historic photographs from the exhibition *The Camera's Coast* to display in this book, why did we decide to surround them with so many other images?

It's the fault of the show's curator, maritime historian Bill Bunting, because he wrote such chatty, engaging labels, loaded to the gills with information about the memorable characters, unfamiliar objects, and bygone activities seen in the photographs. Each photograph has a different story to tell, a story whose every aspect, we realized, could be additionally illustrated by a picture or document drawn from Historic New England's enormous resource of related material ranging from stereo views, boat tickets, and trade cards, to equipment catalogues, yacht designs, and racing schedules. So, instead of producing a standard-format catalogue with one photograph per page, we decided to frame each photograph with other images that would flesh out the story and fill in the details, all carefully articulated in a striking design by Julia Sedykh with Bunting's labels transformed into rope-bound captions.

We could never have taken this approach without the hoarding instinct of William Sumner Appleton, the man who founded the Society for the Preservation of New England Antiquities (now Historic New England) in 1910. A scion of a prominent Boston family, Appleton was descended from a long line of New England pack rats. People back in those days were more likely to store "useless" printed things in attics than to discard them. Appleton was one of the first pack rats to openly delight in these bits of ephemera and to admit that he just couldn't throw anything on paper away. He even started urging others to act that way too. Many of his friends and associates were unsure about his taste or his common sense, but they cooperated by letting him haul their trash away whenever they were moving or housecleaning. Now that "trash" resides in the Library and Archives at Historic New England, providing paper channel markers that allow us to retrace the course of past life along our region's shores.

The process of selecting the "extra" black-and-white and color illustrations—all 175 of them—was a pleasure shared by the author, myself, and our incomparable librarian, Lorna Condon. We were aided and abetted by Library and Archives Committee member Earle G. Shettleworth, Jr., and Lorna's tireless colleague, Emily Novak.

Richard Cheek
Series Editor

INTRODUCTION

John R. Stilgoe

CAMERAS FLOAT COASTWARD. Almost every old family photograph album contains snapshots of children and sand pails, teenagers frolicking in surf or rowing a rental skiff, young couples half blinded by love and half blinded by beach-reflected sun, mothers with infants shaded by makeshift tents, and old-timers ensconced in folding beach chairs, often shielded by umbrellas. Other photographs focus on steamships inshore, fishing trawlers plodding homeward, perhaps a lobster boat working the ledges, now and then a shipwreck or the fragments of one, all images made from recreational spots, all documenting a momentary vacation observation made permanent. Now and then the rummager of attics and antique shops finds other photographs, usually made from ferries or other commercial craft passing parallel to industrial waterfronts, beneath drawbridges, beside shipyards, sweeping professional and holiday-making image-makers just a wee bit offshore. Sometimes the photographs lie mixed with memorabilia: the steamship ticket or schedule, vacation map, restaurant menu, advertising label, or other ephemera that people picked up, brought home, and preserved as they did shells, rounded stones, and sea glass gleaned from beaches. Taken together, arranged and rearranged, juxtaposed and analyzed, they form a kaleidoscopic vision here momentarily fixed.

Coastal photographs often depict people holding cameras or binoculars, the post-1900 replacement for pocket telescopes. Cameras and binoculars appear not as accessories, not as tiny pails and shovels, toy sailboats, and beach towels, but as something more serious, almost more determined. From time immemorial, alongshore people have gazed out to sea, judging the weather, hoping to spot returning vessels, maybe lifting their eyes up not to the hills but to the shifting low horizon. Always some look coastwise too, up and down the beach, along the edge where sea and land fitfully touch. They look and they have always looked, intently, in a way peculiar to the coast, one that adopted photography almost from its invention. Perhaps the alongshore light welded in a flash to the new image-fixing technique, maybe the openness of water somehow dovetailed with depth-of-field subtleties. Whatever the technological reasons, people brought cameras to the coast.

Many of the images collected here strike contemporary viewers as quiet, not so much precisely composed as meditated and serious, and somehow peaceful, evocative of another era. The subjects, human and otherwise, seem posed, and indeed photographers posed and composed everything as often as they could. Early photographers, professionals and determined, usually wealthy amateurs, understood that chemistry made recording fast-moving subjects impossible. Alongshore, slow glass-plate photography necessarily avoided flying gulls, breaking surf, and people and horses trotting along the strand. Instead photographers recorded salt hayers momentarily stopped "for the camera," picnickers and sidewalk pedestrians posed and waiting for the shutter click, a farmer and his oxen still for a second. But the blurred ox tail and blurred pedestrians striding along T Wharf in 1902 memorialize the difficulty of capturing movement, even with most movement artificially halted so photographers might freeze it forever. In many of the older images collected here, the wind seems still, the workers temporarily absent or stiff, the sea calm: photographic technology dictated photographer love of stillness. Photographers posed their subjects, perhaps a man sitting on a beached boat against a backdrop of a boat moored in mirror-flat water, children around a barrel-wheeled wheelbarrow, or a parasol-shaded woman and friend beneath cedar trees distorted by prevailing wind, and when they could not pose the people before them, often returned to shipyards and other industrial places on Sundays, set up their cumbersome equipment, and worked intently at photographing temporary stillness.

Advertising imagery capitalized on the photographic penchant for stillness. Painters producing images to be lithographed or otherwise mass reproduced delighted in depicting flags and long skirts blowing in the wind, waves washing hair-coloring products ashore, smoke wafting from factories, and pipe-smoking dorymen retrieving longlines from a choppy offshore Atlantic. While photographers delighted in stopped windmills and trolley cars (or the empty trolley track abutting Newburyport clam-digger shacks), they struggled to make decent images of trolleys accelerating away from them, battleships surging across their lenses, or even a coastal steamer slowing to dock. Advertising artists knew no such limitations. For them detailing movement came as naturally as depicting mermaids, the capture of sperm whales, and children playing with July Fourth flags and firecrackers, and even their stillest images often show a trace of movement. Beyond the boiled lobster blows the cannery smoke still, but photographers sometimes chose ice-bound ships, the frozen rigging perfect for the photographic process focused on stillness.

More than technology explains the juxtaposition between images too thoughtlessly called still photographs nowadays and the action-packed hand-drawn advertising images. Many of the photographs originate in documentary efforts understood at the moment of image-making to be important then and for posterity too. From the first photographs collected here to the last, the seriousness of recording suffuses the stillness of stopped work. Until well into the twentieth century, when George Eastman made Kodak snapshot imagery commonplace, making a photograph proved exacting and expensive. Professionals and amateurs aimed cameras carefully, often at what they or clients or friends considered important, and the images that follow record the extraordinary importance of work. From the efficient chute of the lobster-canning factory circa 1870, to the early 1880s portrait of George H. Donnell, to the photographs and stereographs of United States Navy sailors, to the surfboat crew at Orleans, this collection documents alongshore work. In the twenty-first century, few family albums include a single image of parents, even grandparents at work, but all alongshore before the 1920s, photography documented the importance of physical effort, and such photographs often survived because subsequent generations valued the record of industry.

No matter how hard at work at any given point at any given moment, however, the coast has always attracted the idle. Loafing alongshore figures in the first words of Melville's *Moby-Dick,* in the description of weekend loafers lounging on quiet New York wharves, staring down harbor. It figures in much earlier work too, in early nineteenth-century paintings mingling scenery, fine vessels (perhaps owned by those who commissioned the paintings), and men hard at work—but almost always watched by idle women (usually in pairs) and sometimes by idle men. Sometimes a boy, sometimes an elderly man, the idler appears from nowhere to grab a mooring line flung wharf-ward from an incoming vessel. He appears from the shade of a fish shack to explain the whereabouts of the harbormaster, or from the sunny lee of a warehouse to explain that bait is in short supply. While boys and old men congregated at nineteenth-century general stores and at small-town depots at train time, the alongshore idler pioneered the way for poets, artists, frazzled businessmen, and around 1850, women, at least respectable women who walked beaches in groups, sometimes using pretexts, say gathering beach plums for jelly. The idlers brought cameras too.

Walking along beaches, especially on weekends, provided recreation, exercise, and often a wider view than many people had from back porches, farm fields, and small-town, even city streets opening on public parks. But the coast inveigled too. It offered fresh air, coolness in hot summer, and invariably something exotic, not merely alien or foreign. All alongshore landsmen encountered something different, often intelligible after a bit of thought, but often puzzling, and literally scented with romance. The smell of fish, the scent of Stockholm tar, the aroma of low tide, and other coastal odors merely heightened the visual feast of the exotic near home. Every image here rewards sustained scrutiny. Every image provides details that stall the scrutinizer, that produce novelty, that make clear how much people looked at the coast and wondered at it, especially in the era before

Hollywood cinema and television redirected attention to programmed, kinetic imagery.

Casually encountering the exotic, especially in the era when now-sleepy towns like Waldoboro in Maine boasted Federal custom houses because they received ships from around the world, produced a sort of casual intellectual dalliance that welded with romantic art. In the pages that follow here the acute scrutinizer must necessarily encounter not only thoughts but feelings and similitudes of feelings. So often the images make the observer think, about overall patterns, tiny details, and perhaps chiefly, the uses of items in larger processes now drifting beyond memory. But very frequently the images produce feelings too. Often the scenes seem quiet, and scrutinizing the images produces feelings—or something akin to genuine emotions—of relaxation, of casual, value-free visual analysis not made fast to any workaday need to obtain the right answer quickly and not rushed along by cinematic or video programming. Much here is immediately mysterious, but not threatening. Rather, it beguiles. Much here is most definitely hard work stopped by the camera, but work that somehow invites the viewer into it, and then beyond, and much concerns re-creational idleness, the relaxation that re-creates the psyche. Much is what ordinary people, especially determined amateurs equipped with superb cameras, found romantic in a way peculiar to the coast. Much of it proves almost dreamlike.

Why else photograph *City of Bangor* sunk at a Boston pier in 1934? The vessel is not some ancient sailing ship that once traded to Shanghai or even Santiago, but a coastal steamer become derelict. The ship, the scene, and now the image become romantic in ways that still defy analysts of contemporary American aesthetics. The well-composed image gently seduces the viewer into musing at the modern cranes atop the pier, then into wondering how long the sunken derelict has stymied cargo transfer, then into musing on the quietude of a port in the Depression. Nowadays Americans stare raptly at fishing boats offloading their catch in Scituate, Massachusetts, and in a hundred other ports, and they make electronic images of the fish, the fishermen, and the often rusted fishing boats. Never do they turn and photograph the often rusted refrigerator trucks into which truckers load the iced, boxed fish. The rusted fishing boat remains romantic, it and its crew somehow exotic, but the truck rusted from dripping salt water is merely a truck, neither romantic nor photogenic, and no longer does anyone call its driver a teamster. In the 1870s, a complex cultural process produced an inchoate license to photograph alongshore things, and the advertising depicted in the ephemera that follow only strengthened it.

The somehow romantic coast drew the attention of photographers who rarely relaxed by ambling along streets abutting gas works, paint factories, oil refineries, slaughterhouses, and other industrial locales every bit as active and prosperous as those they found alongshore. Families picnicked not beside aromatic abattoirs or coal-smoke-scented railroad yards, but they settled down next to all sorts of momentarily quiescent alongshore industry, and often they made a photograph or four. The coast invited thoughtful observers long before the invention of photography, but the great concentration of American population along the Atlantic seaboard helped insure that each generation continued to visit, loaf, and look, and make photographs that now entrance any thoughtful observer of the images that follow here. Kodak and other film-manufacturer advertising taught Americans to carry box cameras to the coast, to make snapshots that often appear fuzzy and ill composed, but by then Americans already visited the coast, looked around, and returned again and again to make far more astute images with far more sophisticated cameras.

Turn these pages deliberately then, read the captions more than once, see the images in the context of other images on other pages, and then ask why someone made any particular image. Sometimes the answer seems clear. Professionals made some images to record something— usually enterprise momentarily paused—permanently, for the future perhaps, and the future is momentarily now. Amateurs documented scenes and people of cultural or personal importance. But often the answers prove much more elusive, and asking and asking again proves an ever more rewarding imaginative exercise in understanding the peculiar eye Americans have for the coast.

Author of *Alongshore, Lifeboat,* and many other books, John R. Stilgoe is Orchard Professor in the History of Landscape at Harvard University.

Clam Diggers, Provincetown, Mass.

THE
CAMERA'S COAST

OLD PHOTOS CONVEY the magic and power of photography as perhaps no others can. They not only allow us to view a world that has vanished but provide us with a better perspective from which to view the world of today.

The Camera's Coast, based on an exhibition of the same name, presents images of coastal life from Historic New England, which holds one of the world's outstanding collections of historic maritime photographs. In the book, colorful ephemera and other related documents surround the photographs, providing an added layer of information and period flavor.

The late nineteenth and early twentieth centuries were times of great social and economic change. Along New England's coast, many traditional maritime and rural occupations declined or vanished. Although major harbors bustled, and coastal shipping boomed, many once important smaller ports became but rustic backwaters. As industrial cities grew crowded, hot, and dirty, increasing numbers of well-off residents removed to coastal resorts for the summer. Yachting blossomed. People of lesser means sought relief through brief shore excursions.

Today, while more people than ever before live along the New England coast, relatively few know the state of the tide, note the direction of the wind, or make their livings on the water or the waterfront. We drive over or under waterways rather than ferry across them. Views and vistas from shoreline roads have vanished with reforestation, and traditional access to the water is blocked by shoreline subdivision, new cottages and castles, and No Trespassing signs. Indeed, the coast of the past, as presented through photographs, is in many ways more accessible, more vital, more interesting, and even more familiar than is the coast of today.

KEY TO IMAGES

Each of the seventy-five main photographs is printed in duotone within a two-page spread and is marked "a," unless it is a full bleed. The supporting illustrations are printed in color or black and white and are lettered consecutively from top to bottom, beginning with the left-hand page. For additional information about each image, see the "Illustration Sources and Bibliography" at the back of the book. All of the images are from the collection of Historic New England unless otherwise noted in the back matter.

Lobster Canning Factory, Mount Desert, Maine, c. 1870

E. L. Allen (active 1860s–1890s)

a

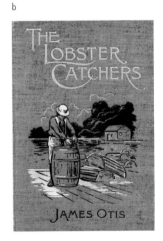

b

c

CASTINE PACKING CO.
PENOBSCOT BAY
CASTINE, ME. U.S.A.

GREETINGS FROM MAINE

MOUNT KATAHDIN FROM KIDNEY POND

4832-29

THE CANNING OF MAINE LOBSTER meat began about 1850 in Portland, which soon became the center of a great canning industry, putting up a variety of products. Under pressure from the many factories, stocks of lobsters, once so plentiful as to be considered a bait-stealing nuisance by cod fishermen, were greatly diminished. By the early 1890s, scarcity, regulations, and competition from the live lobster trade had caused the removal of Maine's lobster canning industry to Canada.

An enduring legacy of the now all but vanished canning industry of Maine is Baxter Park, established by Percival Baxter, a scion of the family that owned the Portland Packing Company, the industry leader.

e

Castine Ferry, Bagaduce River, Hancock County, Maine, c. 1896

A. H. Folsom (active 1860s–1900s)

THE NORTH CASTINE-WEST BROOKSVILLE FERRY was operated by a Mr. Jones and his daughter Sadie. Sadie stands in what is at present the bow; Jones poses aft with his sculling sweep. With a fair breeze the mast and sail lying beyond the team could be used. The long, springy buckboard was developed for the booming Mt. Desert summer tourist trade. Biggest models seated fourteen.

Before the Civil War, Castine outfitted hundreds of area fishing schooners. Her square-riggers carried salt fish—no doubt much was food for slaves—to New Orleans, there to be exchanged for cotton for England and Europe. Ships returned with more salt for preserving more fish. But by the 1890s, the waterfront was empty, and older residents sat in their big houses clipping coupons, dreaming of a railroad to Canada that would boom the old port.

Thin-soiled Brooksville—"Coasterville"—spawned many sailors. In the 1880s and '90s, wealthy Bostonians entertained the locals by purchasing poor land simply for its views. In August, 1888 a Bangor paper reported that in three months time over $40,000 had been paid for Brooksville land which "was not earning a cent."

Cobbler, Isle Au Haut, Eastern Penobscot Bay, Maine, c. 1896

S. I. Carpenter (dates unknown)

a

b

c

THE FOLLOWING appeared in the Belfast, Maine, *Republican Journal*, June 1896,

The queerest looking craft that has visited these waters for a long time arrived in port last Friday. It is a small scow built this past winter at Swan's Island by Capt. William Cottle, who makes his home on board and earns his livelihood by going from place to place doing odd jobs of cobbling . . . . Capt. Cottle is lame and uses crutches to get aboard. His only shipmate is a small yellow dog. He calls his vessel the Yankee Notion.

Cottle's little yellow dog was named Snips. A motley fleet of sloops, catboats, schooners, and even a small steamer or two carried a variety of opportunists and hucksters who targeted isolated coastal folk in general, and islanders in particular.

Cottle's single-minded enterprise—his wife and daughter elected to remain ashore after a trial cruise—was in the finest Yankee tradition. Generations of New England farm families had cut and stitched and pegged away through long winters making shoes for jobbers. Then came shoe shops, followed by increasingly clever machinery, and ever bigger factories. Massachusetts, in particular, and New England, in general, became the nation's shoemakers.

But as time passed on, there came a day
When buckles and finery passed away,
And the patriot held that the proper things
Were home-made shoes with leather strings.

THE STETSON SHOE

THE STETSON SHOE

In full black boots the officer stood
Who led his troops for their country's good,
And he lives today in prose and rhyme,
The beau ideal of that stirring time.

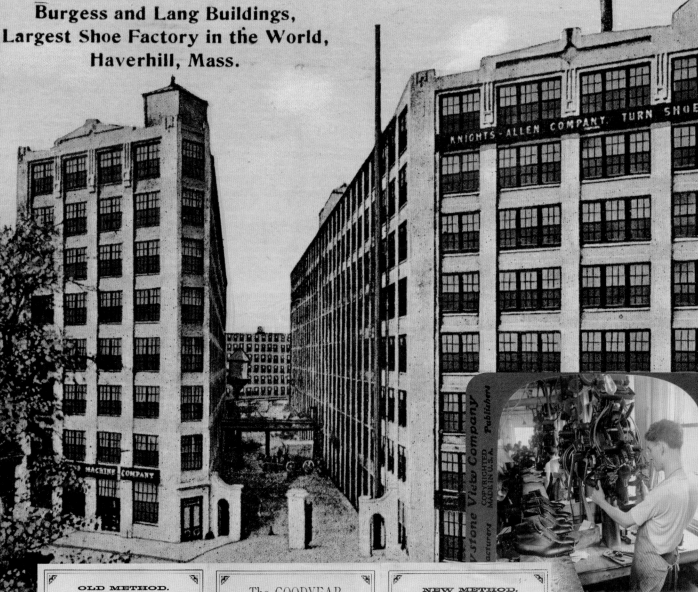

Burgess and Lang Buildings, Largest Shoe Factory in the World, Haverhill, Mass.

d

e

OLD METHOD.

3 PAIRS A DAY.

THE above is a familiar picture of the method still pursued in making hand-sewed welted Shoes, showing no material advance in the process practiced by the Egyptians over 3,000 years ago.

This is the most tedious and laborious work performed by any class of workmen, and it has been considered impossible to accomplish it by machinery until the invention and perfection of the GOODYEAR MACHINE.

Always inquire for the Goodyear Machine-Sewed Welted Shoes.

The GOODYEAR BOOT & SHOE SEWING MACHINES

will be in operation at the Model Shoe Factory of Stribley & Co., at the Cincinnati Industrial Exposition, Sept. 6 to Oct. 7, 1882, affording to all parties an opportunity of witnessing the operation of these machines, and the process of preparing and finishing the work in all its details. Retailers who send in their orders promptly to Stribley & Co. can have sample cases of women's and misses' fine shoes made at the Exposition, at the following prices:—

Women's Fine French Kid Button, per pair,		$4.00 & $4.25
" Curacoa " "		3.10 & 3.60
" Tampico Br'l Oil, Straight Grain,		3.00 & 3.25
" " " " Pebble,		2.75 & 3.00

Each retailer who sends an order for sample dozen by the middle of September, will be furnished with 1,000 of these circulars with his own business card printed on this page, free of charge.

NEW METHOD.

300 PAIRS A DAY.

Goodyear Machine-Sewed Welted Shoes.

Warranted Equal to Hand-sewed.

The distinctive feature of the Goodyear Machine is a curved needle and awl working in a very small circle. This exists in no other machine and is indispensable. Owing to the nature of the work no machine with a straight needle is or can be really practical.

Always inquire for the Goodyear Machine Welted Shoes.

Camden, Maine, c. 1900

Photographer unknown

a

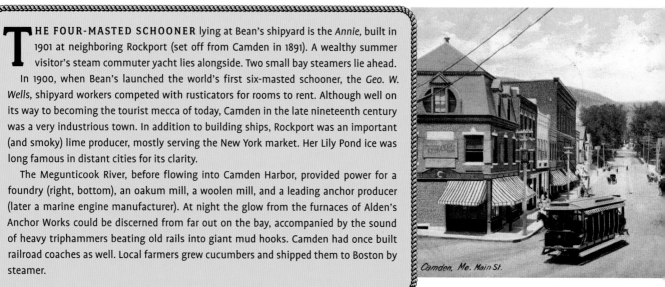

THE FOUR-MASTED SCHOONER lying at Bean's shipyard is the *Annie,* built in 1901 at neighboring Rockport (set off from Camden in 1891). A wealthy summer visitor's steam commuter yacht lies alongside. Two small bay steamers lie ahead. In 1900, when Bean's launched the world's first six-masted schooner, the *Geo. W. Wells,* shipyard workers competed with rusticators for rooms to rent. Although well on its way to becoming the tourist mecca of today, Camden in the late nineteenth century was a very industrious town. In addition to building ships, Rockport was an important (and smoky) lime producer, mostly serving the New York market. Her Lily Pond ice was long famous in distant cities for its clarity.

The Megunticook River, before flowing into Camden Harbor, provided power for a foundry (right, bottom), an oakum mill, a woolen mill, and a leading anchor producer (later a marine engine manufacturer). At night the glow from the furnaces of Alden's Anchor Works could be discerned from far out on the bay, accompanied by the sound of heavy triphammers beating old rails into giant mud hooks. Camden had once built railroad coaches as well. Local farmers grew cucumbers and shipped them to Boston by steamer.

Camden, Me. Main St.

b

c

d

e   **19**

b

LAUNCHING A "SIX MASTER", BATH, ME.

c

pars of Oregon fir finished by hand, ship-yard, Rockland, Me.
© Underwood & Underwood U-19703

d

THE FULL-RIGGED SHIP *HOTSPUR,* of New Bedford, Massachusetts, puts to sea from Boston on her maiden voyage. A sailor stands atop the fore-royal yard, which is being hoisted very likely to the sound of a drunken chantey. Built at Bath, Maine, *Hotspur* was of the final generation of American square-riggers, arguably among the finest and handsomest ever built. For another quarter-century, big schooners would fill Bath's ways.

In 1885, Maine yards produced over half of the wooden tonnage built in the United States, and of that amount, Bath built one-third. Most of the wood and all of the iron used to build ships in Maine came from elsewhere—skilled low-cost labor and deep tradition kept yards active.

Hotspur is bound for Melbourne, via the Cape of Good Hope, carrying a general cargo. She would make a fast passage of eighty-two days. On her second voyage she was lost on an East Indian reef, the fate of uncounted ships before her.

Biddeford Pool, Maine, c. 1880

Baldwin Coolidge (1845–1928)

AN ARTFUL ARRANGEMENT OF FISHERMEN'S GEAR, from wheelbarrow to dory and everything in between includes a stone "killick" anchor, cod handlines, clam hoe and clam hod, tub of trawl, fyke net, gill net, various buoys, lobster traps, harpoon, oars, lunch "kid," dip-net, trawl gurdy, gaff, water jug, boat bailer, and so on.

Located at the mouth of the Saco River, Biddeford Pool in 1880 was a settlement of several hundred inhabitants. The mile-square "pool" was accessible even at high tide only to small to medium-sized vessels, most being engaged in taking cod, hake, haddock, and pollock on handlines. Also, lobsters were trapped and clams were dug. A municipal ordinance—not strictly enforced—outlawed the sale of any clams, they being intended for local use as bait or sustenance.

George H. Donnell, York, Maine, early 1880s

Emma L. Coleman (1853–1942)

YPE

Copper Alloy Type, Self-spacing Type, and all the latest productions in Job
Type; Brass Rule, Metal Furniture, Cuts, Borders, Ornaments, Black and
Colored Inks, Gold and Silver Bronzes, Celluloid and Holly Wood Type, etc.
We carry a greater variety of Type in stock than any foundry in this country

—Send 10 Cents for Complete Illustrated Catalogue; 10 Cents for
d Type Catalogue; and 25 Cents for Book of Engravings.

<a

TOWER'S

MARK.

FISH BRAND

SLICKERS

— AND —

LED CLOTHING

iled Hats and Horse Cover

— MANUFACTURED BY —

J. TOWE

Cor.

ke Tre

H. C. D.

— MA

SEL

Hand Sta

COPYRIGHT, 1901, BY DETROIT PHOTOGRAPHIC CO.

8640. A CAPE ANN FISHERMAN.

c

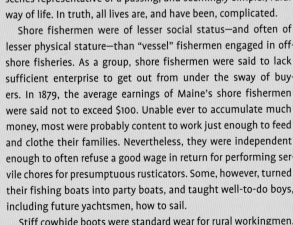

MAN AND DORY.

COPYRIGHT, 1905, BY DETROIT PHOTOGRAPHIC

d

D ONNELL, A "SHORE" FISHERMAN and lobsterman, stands artfully posed by photographer Emma Coleman. Vernacular photographers like Coleman, responding to increased industrialism and urbanization, sought to depict scenes representative of a passing, and seemingly simpler, rural way of life. In truth, all lives are, and have been, complicated.

Shore fishermen were of lesser social status—and often of lesser physical stature—than "vessel" fishermen engaged in off-shore fisheries. As a group, shore fishermen were said to lack sufficient enterprise to get out from under the sway of buyers. In 1879, the average earnings of Maine's shore fishermen were said not to exceed $100. Unable ever to accumulate much money, most were probably content to work just enough to feed and clothe their families. Nevertheless, they were independent enough to often refuse a good wage in return for performing servile chores for presumptuous rusticators. Some, however, turned their fishing boats into party boats, and taught well-to-do boys, including future yachtsmen, how to sail.

Stiff cowhide boots were standard wear for rural workingmen. The fish, perhaps pollock, may be destined to become lobster bait. A severe shortage of bait was but one of many complications in the lives of shore fishermen.

b

R & SON,

OF —

CLOTHING,

NERS' HATS.

FACTORY:

THORNDIKE ST.,

Rear of Second, East Cambridge.

OFFICE IN BOSTON:

45 BROAD STREET.

EXHIBITION

DELPHIA, MDCCCLXXVI

Covers.

Clamming, York River, Maine, c. 1890

Fred Quimby (1862-1896)

a

b

c

No. 1218.   New England Clam Bake.

The only Genuine
R. I. CLAM BAKE

SERVED EVERY DAY,

Arlington Ho
STRAWBERRY HILL

Dinner from 12 M. to 6

BILL OF FAR

Baked Clams, with melted butte
Clam Chowder,   Fried Pe
Baked Blue Fish,   Nantask
Clams in Batter,   Sweet Potatoes
Green Corn,   Chilled Melons,
Cucumbers,

Tea or Coffee, and Bread.

DINNER TICKETS, 50c.

Children under 10 years, half price.

S. L. CHESSMAN, & CO, Prop's.

B EFORE THE TWENTIETH-CENTURY INVASION of the voracious alien green crab, clams were wonderfully abundant. Astonishingly large quantities of shucked meats were salted in barrels for use as bait by New England fishermen as well as canned for human consumption. Clam bait was even exported to Spain and Portugal. The rise of summer tourism opened up a new market for steamed clams served with shore dinners.

In some coastal communities, the consumption of clams carried a social stigma, clams having long served as a dietary fallback for the poor. Indeed, it was said that in some towns only the very rich and the very poor openly ate clams. During the Civil War, clams sustained many families whose men were gone.

Farmer Loading his Cart with Kelp, Long Sands, York, Maine, 1882

Emma L. Coleman (1853–1942)

a

b

RICH IN MINERALS, KELP was used as fertilizer. Farmers also dug large quantities of fertilizing "mussel mud," which, after freezing, dried to a light powder. The ownership of seaweed and mud was regulated by ancient laws. Thoreau watched no-nonsense farmers of Cohasset, Massachusetts, amongst the rubbish and corpses cast ashore from a wrecked immigrant brig "busily collecting the seaweed which the storm had cast up, though they were often obliged to separate fragments of clothing from it."

The beaches at York early attracted the construction of massive hotels. Summer resorts gave local farmers a good market for produce (particularly fresh butter), for extra bedrooms, and for real estate. The ox cart, now all but forgotten, was perhaps the most important land vehicle over hundreds of years of New England history. The oxen are Ayrshires, a hardy, active Scottish dairy breed known for being "high-horned, high-lifed, and thin-skinned."

ork Beach, Me., York Beach and Union Bluff

York, Me., Hotel Albracca.

Salt-Marsh Haying, Hampton, New Hampshire, c. 1890

C. M. Turner (dates unknown)

a.1

The Marshes, Plum Island, Newburyport, Mass.

b

Salt haying, Polpis, Nantucket

c

> **S**ALT HAY WAS STORED IN RAIN-SHEDDING STACKS built atop cedar post "staddles." The natural grasslands of coast and rivers were centers of early European settlement, and for more than two centuries "marshing" was an annual ritual. Haying was timed to the moon's apogee, when tides were lowest. Mowing was mostly by hand. Hay was "poled" to the staddles on long poles carried by two men—stopping to swat accursed greenhead flies before the staddle was reached was forbidden. Cattle relished the salty hay, although it was said that more fat was carried onto the marshes than was ever carried off. Salt-marsh hay was also used as packing material and as stable and strawberry bedding.

Gundalow *Fanny M,* Dover, New Hampshire, November 27, 1896

Nathaniel L. Stebbins (1847–1922)

GUNDALOWS WERE shoal, broad cargo carriers, well-suited for employment in their home waters. They were sailed, rowed and poled. The exotic-looking lateen rig allowed the gundalows to squeeze under low bridges. The great spruce spar, almost seventy feet long, was counter-balanced at the butt; the stump mast, which turned on its step, was canted slightly to port. A single leeboard was fitted to port.

Gundalows carried all manner of freight, including hay, produce, manufactured goods, and a great deal of coal brought to the Piscataqua River by schooner and barge. *Gundalow* was a variation on *gondala,* a common term for a scow.

b

08

THE LARGE INDUSTRIAL PLANT on Freeman's Point (in the background of the photograph at right) was the short-lived White Mountain Paper Company. Claimed to be able to make paper from salt water, it made money for only a few from the sale of salted stock.

At left, on the south side of the river, we see the white bow of one of the two four-masted coal schooners in the Boston-based Palmer fleet; the other eleven fleet members were five-masters. An unseen three-master shares the dock. Further to the left, two stubby-masted coastal barges lie alongside each other at the Consolidated Coal Company coal pocket. At far left are two big coastal tugs, normally employed towing strings of coal barges. Schooners and barge lines were great rivals—not only did barges supplant schooners in the trade, but in confined waters the long tows were a great hazard to sailing vessels. The site of the coal pocket is now Prescott Park. The little white steamer doubtless runs to the Isles of Shoals. As was frequently done, the original photograph was reproduced as a color postcard (left, top).

c

COPR. DETROIT PUBLISHING CO.

d

White Island Light, Isles of Shoals, New Hampshire, c. 1905

Henry G. Peabody (1855–1951)

a

A GROUP OF SEVEN ISLANDS located six miles off Portsmouth, the Isles of Shoals were perils to navigation. The original lighthouse was erected in 1821; the brick tower shown here was built in 1855, and the keeper's house in 1877. The tower still stands, although the other buildings have been razed.

This photograph, taken from a Lighthouse Service tender, is a study of balanced composition and bureaucratic good order. Note the keeper aloft on the tower; his boat posed with sail set, lobster traps and dory neatly stored alongside the trim boathouse, and the perfectly posed good dog. In the 1830s and '40s, the father of famed poet, artist, and wildflower gardener Celia Leighton Thaxter was the keeper at White Island. Celia sometimes trimmed and lit the lamps herself. She wrote:

> I lit the lamps in the light-house tower,
> For the sun dropped down and the day was
> dead;
> They shone like a glorious clustered flower,
> Two golden and five red.

Lift up thy light, O Soul, arise and shine,
    Steadfast while all the storms of life assail!
Immortal spark of the great Light divine,
    Against whose power no tempest shall prevail!

Hold high thy lamp above earth's restless tides,
    Scatter thy messages of hope afar!
Falsehood and folly pass, but Truth abides:
    Thine be the splendor of her deathless star.

When the world's sins and sorrows round thee rave
    Pierce thou the darkness with thy dauntless ray,
Send out thy happy beams to help and save,
    "More and more shining to the perfect day"!

Celia Thaxter.

c

d

Salisbury Beach, Massachusetts, 1919

The New England News Company (active c. 1905–1925)

a

b

c

d

e

SHOOTING THE CHUTES AT WONDERLAND, REVERE BEACH, MASS.

NANTASKET
BEACH
and
PLYMOUTH

FREDERIC L. LANE
TREASURER AND
GENERAL MANAGER

MOST AMUSEMENT PARKS existed in symbiotic or subsidiary relationship with trolley or steamboat lines. Salisbury's park was established in 1888 as a destination for excursion steamer passengers. After 1892, a trolley line delivered droves of Merrimack Valley textile workers.

Trolley lines began the rush to the suburbs, gave hope to sleepy burgs bypassed by railroads, and revolutionized personal mobility, particularly for rural women. The automobile, in turn, while widening horizons, made travel so common as to render many once attractive destinations no longer worth visiting and eventually helped to kill the parks.

Amusement park rides leave the rider no farther ahead, yet hopefully satisfied by either a thrilling experience or its cessation. Salisbury's wonderful "Flying Horses" carousel was moved to San Diego in 1976, where it was later sold at auction, future generations of children be damned.

3. Paragon Park, Nantasket Beach, New England. World's Fair $50,000 Creation, 100,000 Electric Lights, 20 Acres.

Aug. 16. 1906

Fish Market, Newburyport, Massachusetts, c. 1870

H. P. Macintosh (1830–1907)

a

b

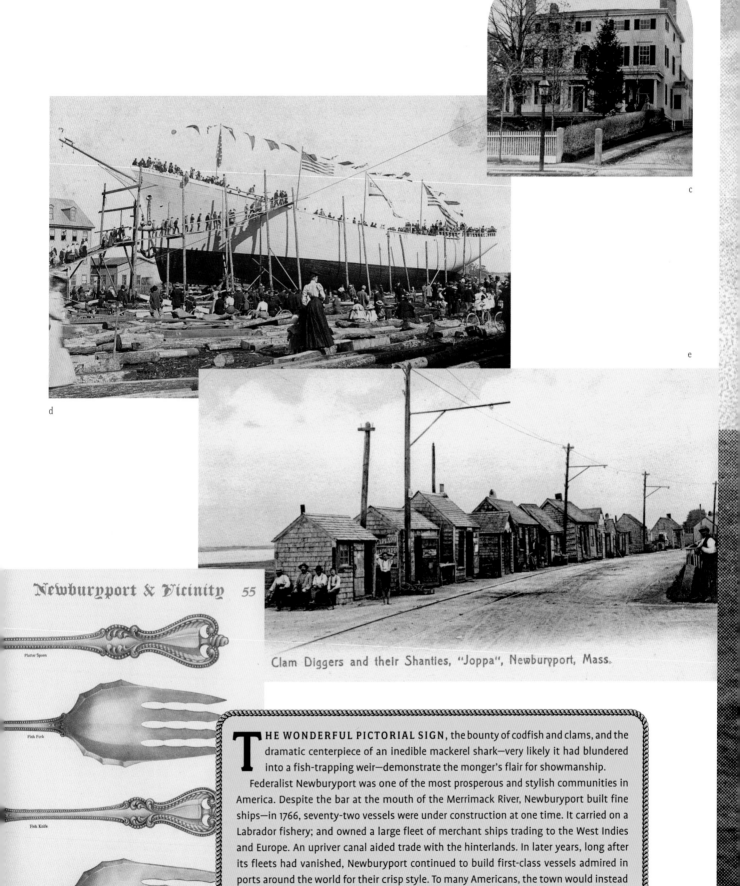

c

e

d

Newburyport & Vicinity 55

Platter Spoon

Fish Fork

Fish Knife

Salad Fork, large

Clam Diggers and their Shanties, "Joppa", Newburyport, Mass.

THE WONDERFUL PICTORIAL SIGN, the bounty of codfish and clams, and the dramatic centerpiece of an inedible mackerel shark—very likely it had blundered into a fish-trapping weir—demonstrate the monger's flair for showmanship.

Federalist Newburyport was one of the most prosperous and stylish communities in America. Despite the bar at the mouth of the Merrimack River, Newburyport built fine ships—in 1766, seventy-two vessels were under construction at one time. It carried on a Labrador fishery; and owned a large fleet of merchant ships trading to the West Indies and Europe. An upriver canal aided trade with the hinterlands. In later years, long after its fleets had vanished, Newburyport continued to build first-class vessels admired in ports around the world for their crisp style. To many Americans, the town would instead be best known as the home of Towle Silversmiths, whose flatware designs were often anything but crisp.

Aero View Map
SHOWING TERRITORY
COVERED BY THE LINES
OF THE
BAY STATE
STREET RAILWAY CO.
AND THEIR CONNECTIONS

Red lines indicate routes
of the Bay State St. Ry Co. cars
Black lines indicate
those of other companies

ISSUED BY THE PASSENGER DEPARTMENT
308 Washington St.   Boston

Copyright Bay State St. Ry. Co. 1912

c

Plum Island, Newburyport, Massachusetts, c. 1905

Thomson and Thomson (active c. 1905–1915)

a

SUMMERTIME—HOT SAND, SHARP-EDGED BEACH GRASS, tiny cottages and boardwalks, Old Glory, a trolley, and a glimpse of the lighthouse marking the treacherous mouth of the Merrimack River. The sea is nowhere to be seen, but is sensed everywhere. No photo of crashing waves could evoke any stronger sense of a beloved, lazy, turn-of-the-century, middle-class seaside summer resort. Nowadays, summer weekend traffic clogs Plum Island's access road, and year-round occupancy of cottages on tiny lots has created a civic conundrum regarding wells and septic systems. Winter storms wreak havoc. But the sea still has magic.

The poster on the trolley advertises "Howe's Great London Shows, Newburyport, Aug. 22." Many theater companies that toured New England in the summer were composed of big city show people on working vacations. Early morning departures from hotels, with bills left behind unpaid, were not unheard of.

< b

d

Nellie Moody, Gloucester, Massachusetts, c. 1890

Photographer unknown

a

b

All claims for allowance must be made at our office within three days from receipt of goods.

TERMS: 30 days or 1 per cent. off if paid within 10 days from date of bill.

· ESTABLISHED 1872 ·

Harvey C. Smith

WHOLESALE

Fish

DEALER.

MANUFACTURER OF BONELESS CODFISH.

CAPE ANN TURKEY AND UNCLE SAM BRANDS A SPECIALTY.

PACKER OF MACKEREL.   SMOKER OF HALIBUT.

OFFICE, REAR 33 MAIN ST.   Gloucester Mass.   Apr. 8th, '02.

Sold to   Mr. W. H. Osgood, Claremont, N.H.

1-36 case C.A.Turkey	13-1/2		4.86
1-36 case Choice Morsels	6-1/2		2.34
1-24 case 1# Famous	10		2.40
1/2 bbl. Salmon			6.85

44

COPYRIGHT, 1906, BY
DETROIT PUBLISHING CO.

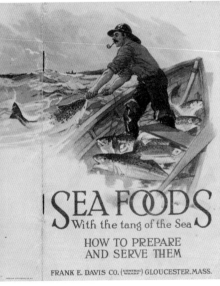

SEA FOODS
With the tang of the Sea

HOW TO PREPARE
AND SERVE THEM

FRANK E. DAVIS CO. (CENTRAL WHARF) GLOUCESTER, MASS.

d

THE LITTLE BARK *NELLIE MOODY* unloads salt at a salt warehouse; some is also being discharged into a smaller craft tied alongside. Built at Green Cove, Nova Scotia, in 1873, the bark hailed from the once great ship-owning port of Yarmouth, Nova Scotia.

Gloucester, the greatest fishing port in the nation, was also the nation's greatest importer of salt; in 1879, 43,102,164 pounds were delivered by sea. Sea salt from Trapani, Sicily, was preferred for preserving fish aboard vessels on the banks, while Liverpool and especially Cadiz salt were used for pickling. Gloucester's fleet then numbered about 440 schooners fishing from Greenland's Davis Strait and the Grand Banks of Newfoundland south to the Virginia capes. Most of this great fleet was built nearby in the little village of Essex.

b

9
WEST STREET

TERRY & COOK AND CO
CHILDRENS BOYS & YOUTHS'
STYLISH
NEW YORK CLOTHING

PURITAN

PURITAN.
Winner of the Queen's Cup. International Regatta, off Sandy Hook, Wednesday, Sept. 16, '85.

THE TRIAL-TRIP.

c

The BOY MECHANIC
BOOK 1
700 THINGS
for
BOYS TO DO
800 ILLUSTRATIONS SHOWING HOW

d

46

a

THE WIDESPREAD POPULARITY of model yachting was enhanced by strong public interest in America's Cup racing. Model yacht building flourished in high school industrial arts classes. The hotbed of model yachting in Massachusetts was Redd's Pond, Marblehead.

Mrs. Greely Curtis, née Harriot Appleton, of Mt. Vernon Street, Boston, and Manchester, took this lovely photograph of two of her ten children. Her father, Nathan Appleton, was a Boston financier and industrialist. The Curtises' great stone seaside "cottage" was but one of many such residences built by wealthy Bostonians along the North Shore's "Gold Coast, " extending from Beverly to Eastern Point, Gloucester, from the 1840s on. One North Shore farmer, overwhelmed by the huge price paid by a wealthy Bostonian for his poor-soiled ocean-front property, threw a yoke of oxen into the deal to assuage his conscience.

Figurehead, Peach's Point, Marblehead, Massachusetts, c. 1915

Mary H. Northend (1850–1926)

CUSTOM HOUSE, BOSTON, MASS.

Friday Aug. 6
Capt Edward Curtis & Capt John Lyons crew —
lipped mornings 4 A.M. wind N Arrived
from Cove 9 A.M. Went into the
, 5. Pile. Took a squall me
SW of White Island. Carried her
it & took in no sail

A FIGUREHEAD, SAID to have belonged to a Nova Scotian bark named *Marie*, planted in Robert Swain Peabody's shorefront garden at his summer estate. "Marie" shared a rose-covered pergola with two more formidable-appearing wooden matrons and a fierce-faced, tomahawk-wielding Indian. Not yet elevated from the status of oversized garden gnomes, figureheads, constructed of white pine, were commonly left to deteriorate outdoors—indeed, a certain degree of decay lent the relics a fashionable air of tragic romance. At the center of the garden was a ship's binnacle, converted to a sundial, that bore the lines of the poet William Robert Spencer, "How noiseless falls/ the foot of time/That only falls on flowers."

Robert Peabody was one of the architects of Boston's Back Bay, whose upscale row houses were not designed for comfort in summer heat, it being assumed that the owners would then be in their summer residences. Boston's first skyscraper, the 1915 tower sprouting from the 1837–47 Customs House, was the work of his firm, Peabody and Stearns. An avid sailor and sketcher of coastal scenes, Peabody bewailed the supplanting of ancient forms of naval architecture by utilitarian modern designs.

< a

b

c

d

49

The Racing Catboat *Koorali*, June 17, 1892

Nathaniel L. Stebbins (1847–1922)

a

b

N. L. Stebbins, Inc.

184 BOYLSTON STREET. BOSTON

Commercial Photographer
Marine Photos

PHONE BEACH 0136 ROOM 54

c

d

N. L. STEBBINS, INC.
E. U. GLEASON, *Mgr.*
A partial list of our 8/10 Photographs of Ships etc.
184 BOYLSTON STREET, BOSTON, MASS.

Name	Rig	View	Wind
Afghanistan	4-mast Bark	Port	Lee in Shadow
Afghanistan	4-mast Bark	Starboard	Windward
Afghanistan	4-mast Bark	Star Quarter	Windward
Apache	Bark. Yacht	Starboard	Lee
Cedar Croft	Bark	Starboard	Windward
Cedar Croft	Bark	Star Quarter	Windward
Dauntless	Ship	Port Side	Lee
Hercules	Ship	Starboard	Lee
Hercules	Ship	Stern	Wind
W. R. Hutchins	Brigantine	Stern	Wind
W. R. Hutchins	Brigantine	Starboard	Lee
Independence	Ship	Port	Lee
Kennard	Bark	Port	Lee
Kennard	Bark	Stern	Wind
Leading Wind	Ship	Starboard	Wind
Leading Wind	Ship	Starboard	Free
Lands Kron	Bark	Starboard	Wind
Pass of Balmaha	Ship	Starboard	Sails Furled
Panay	Ship	Starboard	Lee
Panay	Ship	Port	Lee
Panay	Ship	Bow	Lee
Panay	Ship	Stern	Wind
Paul Jones	Ship	Port	Lee
Rachel Emery	Barkentine	Port	Lee
Rachel Emery	Barkentine	Starboard	Wind
John S. Emery	Barkentine	Starboard	Lee
Rapid Transit	Brigentine	Starboard	Wind
Sarah	Bark	Starboard	Lee
Sarah	Bark	Port	Lee
Sooloo	Ship	Port	Lee
Sooloo	Ship	Port Bow	Lee
...loo	Ship		Wind
...beam	Barkentine Yacht	Starboard	Lee
...'l Schofield	Ship	Port	Lee
...andra	Ship	Port	Lee
...andra	Ship	Starboard	Wind
...falgar	4-mast Ship	Starboard	Bare Poles
...age	Ship (Stuns'ls)	Starboard	Lee
...halla	Ship Yacht	Starboard	Lee
...W. Lawson	7-mast Schooner	Port	Lee Shadow
...W. Lawson	7-mast Schooner	Starboard	Wind Sun
...W. Lawson	7-mast Schooner	Bow	Lee Shadow

THE YACHTSMAN'S ALBUM

FROM PHOTOGRAPHS BY N·L·STEBBINS

e

STEBBINS ILLUSTRATED COAST PILOT

NATHANIEL L. STEBBINS, ACTIVE from 1884 until his death in 1922 at age seventy-five, was primarily employed photographing yachts, although his portraits of commercial vessels are arguably of equal importance. He was an artist and craftsman of high order, often working with his heavy glass-plate camera aboard a rolling tug. He was also a shrewd merchandiser and publisher of his work.

The traditional Cape Cod catboat, with but one sail, was the essence of simplicity. The adoption of ever-bigger mainsails for racing in the 1890s necessitated the addition of a balancing jib, along with the "excrescence" of a bowsprit. Hulls were subjected to tremendous torque. The heaviest crewman was usually the mainsheet tender, while the most agile shook out the reefs in the near thousand-square-foot mainsail while tiptoeing back from the end of the forty-foot boom. The leading racing cat builders were the Crosbys, of Osterville, Massachusetts, and C. C. Hanley, *Koorali*'s creator and a Maine native, of Monument Beach (later of Quincy), Massachusetts.

f

Constellation, June 27, 1901

Nathaniel L. Stebbins (1847–1922)

12566-Constellation

THIS 1888 IRON CENTERBOARD SCHOONER-YACHT WAS designed by Boston's Edward Burgess. Under the ownership of the Thayer family, she sailed from Marblehead, where she was the pride of the port. Her longtime professional skipper, Captain Nate Watson, was from an old Plymouth fishing family. Watson was one of the most respected professionals on the coast, routinely sailing *Constellation* to her mooring in crowded Marblehead Harbor. His superbly trained crew hailed from a small village in Norway, to which they returned every winter. Here, three sailors out on the bowsprit prepare to take in the big jib-topsail as the breeze freshens.

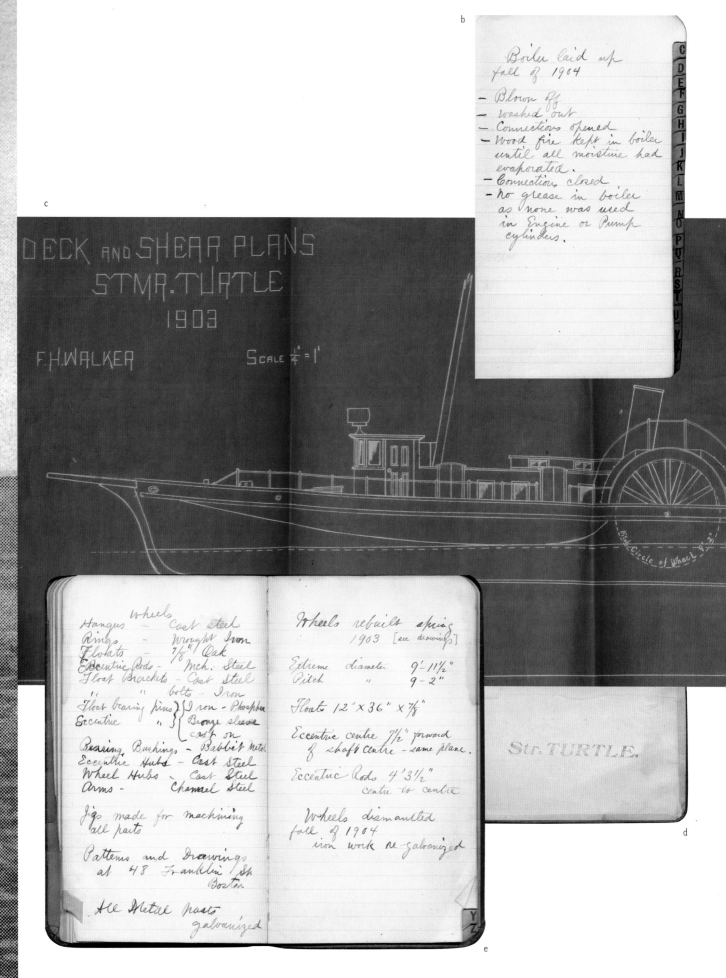

b

Boiler laid up
fall of 1904

- Blown off
- washed out
- Connections opened
- Wood fire kept in boiler
  until all moisture had
  evaporated.
- Connections closed
- No grease in boiler
  as none was used
  in Engine or Pump
  cylinders.

C D E F G H I J K L M N O P Q R S T U V W

c

DECK and SHEAR PLANS
STMR. TURTLE
1903

F.H. WALKER   SCALE ¼" = 1'

Pitch Circle of Wheel 9'-2"

d

Str. TURTLE.

e

Wheels

Hangers   -   Cast Steel
Rings   -   Wrought Iron
Floats   -   7/8" Oak
Eccentric Rods - Mch. Steel
Float Brackets - Cast Steel
   "   "   bolts - Iron
Float bearing pins }} Iron - Phosphor
Eccentric   " }} Bronze sleeve
                     cast on
Bearing Bushings - Babbit Metal
Eccentric Hubs - Cast Steel
Wheel Hubs - Cast Steel
Arms -   Channel Steel

Jigs made for machining
  all parts

Patterns and Drawings
  at 48 Franklin St.
             Boston

All Metal parts
      galvanized

Wheels rebuilt spring
        1903 [see drawing]

Extreme diameter   9'-11½"
Pitch   "   9-2"

Floats 12" x 36" x 7/8"

Eccentric centre 7½" forward
   of shaft centre - same plane.

Eccentric Rods 4'-3½"
        centre to centre

Wheels dismantled
fall of 1904
  iron work re-galvanized

Nathaniel L. Stebbins (1847–1922)

a

THIS DELIGHTFUL PORTRAIT of the steam yacht *Turtle* captures most of the owner's party relaxing aft (excepting two adventurers sitting atop the pilothouse), while the two sailors stand a double bow watch.

Steam yachts came in all sizes and styles. The crème de la crème were the big, exquisitely modeled, engineered, and constructed "English" (most were Scottish) yachts. Some others, including miniature ram-bowed warship designs and rare paddlers like *Turtle,* reflected the unusual tastes of owners. *Turtle* was built at Lynn, Massachusetts, in 1889. Boston dry goods merchant Arthur Amory, resident of the Back Bay, was her longtime owner. Originally sixty-six feet long, *Turtle* had grown to ninety-two feet on deck by 1903. Powered by an inclined compound engine, her wheels were of modern feathering design, with "floats" whose angle was adjusted mechanically for efficiency. Her engineer's notebook and construction blueprints provide a window into her mechanics, operation, and upkeep.

A Swampscott Dory, Swampscott, Massachusetts, c. 1890

Charles P. Jeffers and Wardwell (active late 1880s)

a

SWAMPSCOTT DORIES WERE nearly round-sided but had sufficient flat bottom to stand on a beach. Swampscott was located near wonderfully productive winter fishing grounds, and for many years Fisherman's Beach was the site of a great market, with buyers coming from as far as Canada. Dories were employed fishing and also landing the catch from a fleet of small schooners which anchored off the beach. The town's Yankee fishermen stubbornly stuck with handlines, holding that the multi-hooked trawls used by Irish and Italian boat fishermen and North Shore "shore" fishermen would wipe out the fish stocks.

In the 1890s, "clipper" Swampscott dories became a popular recreational racing craft. Larger dories, fitted with a single cylinder engine, were developed for fishing and pleasure. The dory pictured under sail is being steered with an oar held over the side, the oar being pressed against the side by water pressure. To adjust the course, the oar handle was rotated. Rudders were fitted to dories sold as pleasure craft.

b

R. T. DODGE & CO.

Manufacturers and Dealers in

OARS, SWEEPS, & SCULLS,

No. 176 Commercial Street,

BOSTON.

☞ All kinds of SPRUCE OARS made to order. ☜

E. Gerry Emmons,
Manufacturer of
Sail and Row Boats.
3 New Ocean St. Dories, Skiffs, Etc.
TERMS: F. O. B.
SWAMPSCOTT, MASS. July 2

Sold to Bertie Stuart

Sailing Dory with pump spars etc		$133.
1 — Skiff $10, 1 pr oars $1.		11.—
1 Dory $25. Rowlocks 3.05		28.05
6 lbs. paint .96 2½ hours labor .75		1.71

c

d

Swampscott, Mass.

e

DORY REGATTA.

Swampscot, Aug. 27th, 1859, at 4.30, P. M.

THREE RACES.

Prizes for First Race,—1st Prize, $12 ; 2d Prize, $8.
   "   " Second "   "   "   15 ; "   "   10.
   "   " Grand Scrub Race, $25, and entrance money.

ENTRIES.
FIRST RACE.

CAPS.

Refuge, . . R. H. Derby and R. S. Shelton.   Tricolor.

f

b

INTERIOR OF ROPEWALK, PLYMOUTH CORDAGE COMPANY

SEWALL, DAY & CO'S. CORDAGE MANUFACTORY.
BOSTON, MASS.

d

THE FULL-RIGGED SHIP *PANAY,* of Salem, Massachusetts, departs Boston on June 6, 1887, bound for the Philip-
pines with a cargo including 33,000 cases of kerosene in
tins. She will return in eleven months with 1,437.5 tons of sugar.
Panay was built at East Boston in 1877; in 1889, she was lost on
the Philippine island of Samar. *Panay* and her sisters, *Sooloo* and
Mindoro, were intended for the Philippine hemp trade, which,
pioneered by W. F. Weld, had made Massachusetts an important
rope-maker. The three little ships themselves required an immense
amount of "running rigging" and were among the last products
of Boston's celebrated shipbuilding industry, which once had
led the world. They were also the last members of Salem's once
great fleet of East Indiamen, which had flourished with the spice
trade. People of the East Indies could once have been excused for
thinking that Salem was a country unto its own.

Captain Joseph Luscomb of Salem stands on *Panay*'s poop,
perhaps contemplating the long road ahead. Luscomb was
relieving *Panay*'s regular master, Captain Stephen Bray, Jr., of
Newburyport, for this one voyage.

a

Panay, June 6, 1887

Nathaniel L. Stebbins (1847–1922)

No. *1*

CARGO BOOK

of ship *Agnes*

Capt. *W. F. Ames*

for *Boston*

WARREN & THAYER'S

BOSTON PACKETS.

c

THE FULL-RIGGED SHIP DEPARTS FROM her home port of Boston, bound around Cape Horn for Valparaiso, Chile. No doubt she is carrying general cargo and will return with heavy copper ore or nitrate of soda. Her owners, Hemenway & Browne, succeeded Augustus Hemenway & Co., after Hemenway's death in 1876. Hemenway entered the Chilean-North American trade in the late 1830s and after weathering many difficulties, eventually controlled it. From 1860 to 1874, suffering from "nervous prostration," he retreated to a sanitarium, leaving the management of the firm to a brother. He encouraged his wife to become a leading public benefactor.

Independence was employed in the punishing trade from her launching in 1871 until at least 1896, when she became the Chilean ship *Temuco*. Built at East Boston, her great durability and also her admirable proportions hark back to Boston's great pre-Civil War clipper building heritage.

The rare 1859 cargo book (far left) is a relic of Boston's pre-Civil War sail packet trade with Liverpool. It lists the cubic measurements of items of general freight.

Hesper, East Boston, August 19, 1889

Nathaniel L. Stebbins (1847–1922)

a.1

2702-Hesper

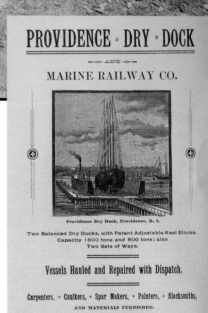

PROVIDENCE · DRY · DOCK

AND

MARINE RAILWAY CO.

Providence Dry Dock, Providence, R. I.

Two Balanced Dry Docks, with Patent Adjustable Keel Blocks.
Capacity 1800 tons and 800 tons; also
Two Sets of Ways.

Vessels Hauled and Repaired with Dispatch.

Carpenters, · Caulkers, · Spar Makers, · Painters, · Blacksmiths,
AND MATERIALS FURNISHED.

P. O. Box, 1284.   A. T. STOWELL, Supt.
TELEPHONE CONNECTION.

THE BOSTON PILOT SCHOONER *Hesper* (above) is readied for a match race with the new fisherman *Fredonia,* with whom she shares the dry dock. *Fredonia,* who had borrowed a mainsail of an America's Cup defender, won handily. *Hesper* had been the standard by which local schooners were rated for speed, whether or not the pilots knew they were engaged in a race. Both schooners represented the evolution towards deeper and more seaworthy hulls, a trend championed by *Hesper*'s designer, D. J. Lawlor, and artfully advanced by Edward Burgess, designer of *Fredonia.*

A small schooner (right, top) is hauled out on a marine railway. The location is not known. Railways were powered by a steam engine or a skinny horse. To move the cradle 160 feet, the horse walked twenty-eight miles.

Boys were tolerated—and indeed often employed—in all manner of nineteenth-century work sites, including boat shops and shipyards. Waterfronts were prime play-grounds for boys; although some drowned, most did not. Despite the fierce prudery then in force, boys customarily swam in the nude, even in relatively public places.

b

MARINE RAILWAY.

To Ship-owners and Masters!

THIS RAILWAY IS ON

SUMNER STREET, . EAST BOSTON,

ADJOINING PEOPLE'S FERRY,

And is the best in the States, lowest prices.

Every description of work appertaining to ve

CARPENTERING, CAULKING, METALING, SHEATHI

done with fidelity and despatch.

In connection there is a good wharf and d
blocks, and on the premises are riggers, pain
block-makers, &c.

A full supply of stock always on hand, and
anteed in all cases. Reference given if require

D. D. KE

J. E. Farwell & Co., Prs., 37 Congress St., Bosto

c

11803 DRY DOCK, PORTSMOUTH NAVY YARD.

d

Pilot Schooner *Varuna*, Boston, 1890s

Photographer unknown

QUINCY BAY

HOUGH'S NECK

MOON ISLAND

A TUG TOWS THE PILOT SCHOONER *Varuna* out of Boston Harbor, passing a loaded stone sloop, probably from Cape Ann, Massachusetts. Stone sloops, based at Cape Ann or Chebeague Island, Maine, were massively built vessels with heavy-lift capacity employed carrying granite coastwise.

Boston's pilot service employed a number of schooners that cruised offshore, competing to place their pilots aboard ships headed for the port. The schooners were fast, weatherly, and able to keep the sea in winter northeasters. One schooner patrolled the harbor entrance to intercept eligible customers—primarily "British" schooners from the Maritime Provinces—that had snuck by the gauntlet. Hungry tugs stationed themselves off Boston Light, while some sought bigger prizes off Race Point, Cape Cod. Likely the tug, like *Varuna*, is heading out to seek prey.

Schooners at Boston's T and Commercial Wharves, 1880s

Baldwin Coolidge (1845–1928)

a

THE SCHOONERS ARE LIKELY ALL FISHERMEN, excepting the packet *Sarah Louise*, of York, Maine, in the foreground, identified as such by her tall after-house, the tiny "caboose" (or portable galley) on deck, and the sign advertising that she is "for Calais," in farthest Down East Maine.

Packets carried freight and passengers between ports on a regular basis. Pre-Civil War Boston had been the center of a great coastal packet trade, and T Wharf was then virtual Maine territory. With the rise in steamers and railroads, the sailing packet business withered, and T Wharf was taken over by fresh-fish dealers. Some Down East packets held on by carrying hazardous cargoes and by serving small communities and timid folk afraid of exploding boilers.

Commercial Wharf was built in the 1830s, and originally housed East Indian, South American, West Indian, Mediterranean, and northern European merchants. No lowly fishing craft would then have tied up there. By the 1870s, it, too, had fallen to the fish dealers.

(C)

ESTABLISHED 1852.

F. D. CHASE

Manufacturer, Wholesale and Retail Dealer in

SHIP CABOOSE STOVES

Cabin Stoves, Ranges, Deck Iron
Ship Lanterns, Marine Lamps
and cooking apparatus of
all kinds.

The undersigned would ask the attention of tho
interested in Shipping to his large stock and asso
ment of Goods in the above line, especially adap
to all sizes and kinds of vessels, from the pleas
yacht to the ocean steamer. Besides my own patte
of ten sizes of Vessels' Stoves, graded in capacity
do the cooking for a crew or company of from fo
persons to four hundred and more if required, I ha
constantly on hand sixteen other different patte
adapted to vessel use.

☞ Special rates made with Ship Builders and others buying any considerable quantity of Goo
at one time.

F. D. CHASE,
221 Commercial Street and 4 Lewis Wharf,
Northerly terminus of Atlantic Avenue,   BOSTON. MASS

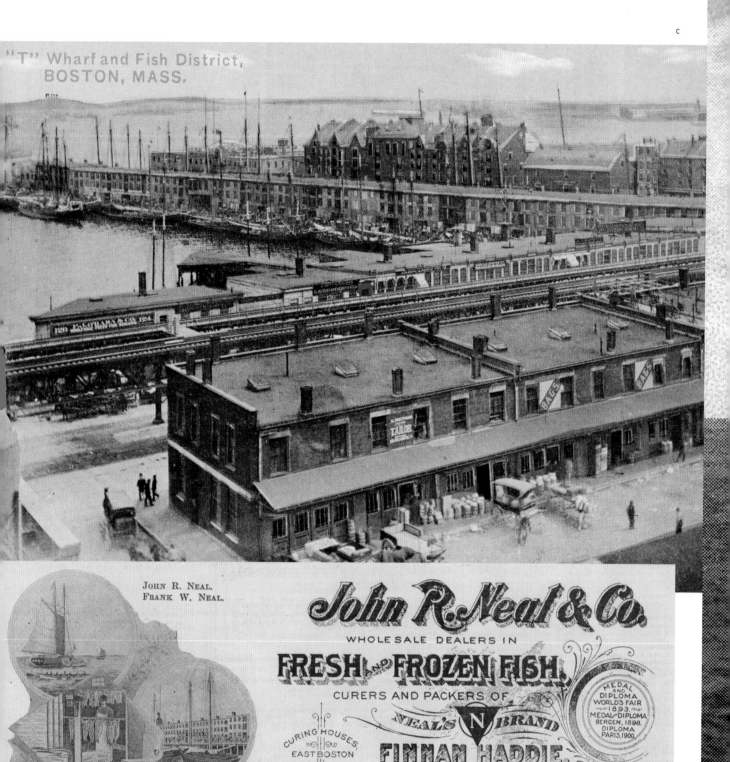

"T" Wharf and Fish District, BOSTON, MASS.

John R. Neal.
Frank W. Neal.

John R. Neal & Co.
WHOLESALE DEALERS IN
FRESH AND FROZEN FISH,
CURERS AND PACKERS OF
NEAL'S N BRAND
CURING HOUSES
EAST BOSTON
FINNAN HADDIE.
21, 22 & 23 T WHARF,
BOSTON, MASS.

MEDAL AND DIPLOMA WORLD'S FAIR 1893. MEDAL-DIPLOMA BERGEN, 1898. DIPLOMA PARIS, 1900.

LONG DISTANCE TELEPHONE.

c

d

Landing a Halibut, T Wharf, Boston, c. 1885

Baldwin Coolidge (1845–1928)

THE GRAND BANKS HALIBUT FISHERY was based at Gloucester, so this schooner is probably a fresh fish trawler, in from George's or Brown's Bank, or from a "shore ground." Trawl fishermen fished from dories, using long trawl lines armed with as many as 1,800 baited hooks. Dories are "nested" in the foreground—hauling such a large fish into a dory was no mean trick.

Note the long main boom, disappearing behind the rigging at far right. With bowsprits and overhanging main booms, the tightly packed schooners at T Wharf frequently "locked horns."

a.1

a.2

MUCH OF PRESENT-DAY BOSTON is filled land, one of the great fill projects in the nineteenth century being the 1869 construction of Atlantic Avenue, which served to connect the northern and southern rail terminals. Created with fill from Fort Hill—the last intact "trimountain" of the old Shawmut peninsula—the project also destroyed the last remnants of the colonial waterfront and bisected great granite warehouses of pre-Civil War maritime commerce. An eclectic hodgepodge of storefronts sprouted along the avenue like opportunistic roadside weeds.

In the view at left, above, we can glimpse the stern and the lofty main mast of the steamer *Bay State*, lying at the harborside remnant of Central Wharf. Her running mate, *Portland*, was lost with all aboard in the terrible gale of November 1898, that would forever bear the name "Portland Gale."

T Wharf, Boston, January 9, 1902

Nathaniel L. Stebbins (1847–1922)

A MOST EVOCATIVE PHOTOGRAPH OF a most interesting place during the most dangerous season for the fishermen. In 1902, ten vessels and eighty-two fishermen were lost from the New England fleet, and surely most were lost during cold-weather months.

After the Civil War, New England's fishing industry underwent a general consolidation from many small ports to several large ports, with Boston becoming the country's leading fresh fish port. T Wharf was the center of the fresh fish business. The larger schooner in the foreground is probably a frequenter of Brown's and George's Banks. She carries long-stocked banks anchors and fiber-cable which could be cut with an axe in an emergency. The smaller schooner to the left, the *Estelle S. Nunan* of Gloucester, is likely a "shore fisherman" employed on the numerous smaller grounds nearer the coast.

Servia, July 31, 1896

Nathaniel L. Stebbins (1847–1922)

b

a.1

Immigration Quarters, East Boston, December 28, 1910

Photograph by the Boston and Albany Railroad Company

c

THE BIG CUNARD PASSENGER LINER (left, bottom) departs from East Boston for Liverpool. Four Boston Tow Boat Company tugs hold her up against a fresh northerly breeze. Note *Servia*'s open bridge—"Mt. Misery"—typical of British ships, and a very cold and unpleasant place when the fast steamer was bucking into a bitter winter northwest gale.

Cunard was the best known of the several major British steamer lines linking Boston to British ports. Eastbound cargo liners carried grain and also livestock—mostly cattle—delivered to Boston by railroads that linked the port to the West.

Above, the immigrants receiving hall at the Cunard Line/Boston & Albany Railroad Pier. In 1907, 131,000 transatlantic passengers entered and cleared from Boston, the great majority being immigrants. White Star Line's new Mediterranean service delivered workers from the south of Italy seeking summer construction jobs.

Fire, East Boston, August 26, 1907

Photograph by the Boston and Albany Railroad Company

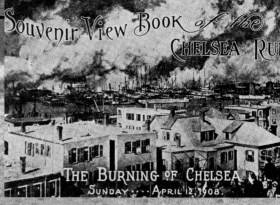

COPYRIGHT,
1906,
BY DETROIT

A FIRE AT AN EAST BOSTON "coal pocket" (left, center). The five-masted schooner is the *Jane Palmer*, built at East Boston in 1904. The *Bangor Daily News* reported:

The five-masted schooner Jane Palmer, *Captain Bowen, caught fire tonight from a blaze which started on the dock of the Massachusetts Wharf Coal Co., alongside of which she was tied, and was badly damaged. The entire after portion of her deck was ablaze at one time and it seemed likely that her cargo of coal, part of which had been discharged, would be destroyed. . . . It was reported that members of the Palmer's crew had been obliged to jump from the vessel and swim across the dock to save themselves . . . . A section of the coal wharf . . . was burned for a distance of 300 feet.*

All of Boston's coal arrived by water; in 1900, coal receipts totaled over four million tons. Coal pockets occupied much of the waterfront. Two steam yachts lie in the foreground at the yacht anchorage near the entrance to the Fort Point Channel.

City of Bangor, Boston, 5 p.m., August 12, 1906

Nathaniel L. Stebbins (1847–1922)

a.1

PASSENGERS EXPERIENCE the thrill of departure as the big side-wheeler (above) departs Foster's Wharf for Maine. Some may later regret the rolling sea off Cape Ann. The steamer will arrive bright and early at Rockland, there to connect with smaller steamers, then to continue on to other Penobscot Bay and river stops before reaching Bangor. (Piloting a big steamer on black and foggy nights was no sinecure.)

Coastal steamer lines were important freight and passenger carriers. Intense rivalries with other lines and also railroads led to corporate collusion, combination, absorption, and confusion. Most of the major lines running from Boston became tentacles of the Eastern Steamship Company. Weakened by rivals, including motor vehicles, coastal steam was finished off by the Second World War. *City of Bangor,* once known as the "Floating Gold Mine," had by then already met her demise. She is shown, at far right, in 1934 in her East Boston deathbed, hard by her birthplace.

b

c

City of Bangor Sunk, Federal Wharf, East Boston, April 19, 1934

R. L. Graham (active 1930s–1960s)

d

e

a.2

The Boston-East Boston Ferry *Noddle Island,* November 2, 1911

Photographer unknown

a.1

b

PILOTHOUSE EAGLES LEND a touch of theater to the begrimed and utilitarian municipal functionary they have alighted upon (above, top). In 1890, Boston's two city-operated ferry lines carried over 900,000 horse-drawn vehicles. Winches installed at the shoreside ramps mercifully assisted the low tide debarkation of wagons, which had been overloaded to save on fares. In the winter, a base of snow was maintained on deck for sleighs and pungs.

Newly built of wood at Chelsea, Massachusetts, the tug *Saturn* (at right, bottom) likely has a hand-me-down engine—wooden hulls wore out, but engines did not. The plume of steam reveals it to be a high-pressure, single-cylinder, non-condensing engine. Such engines were inexpensive and quick responding but required a re-supply of boiler water on a timely basis. And when the engine was started, bystanders were treated to a shower of warm "spit." Because long deckhouses interfered with towing agility, tugs were lashed alongside their charges in confined waters.

c

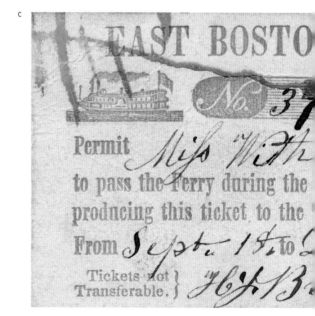

d

e

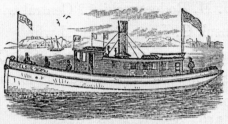

BOSTON TOW-BOAT COMPANY

Tugs.	Captains.
C. M. Winch,	H. McDonald.
L. A. Belknap,	Frank Riley.
Elsie,	George D. Frost.
Camilla,	L. S. Cates.
Emily,	A. L. Stubbs.
Curlew,	E. W. E. Cates.
Vim,	D W. Baker.
Argus,	George W. Taylor.
J. G. Neafie,	Jas. Mooney.
Despatch,	Jos. Hallett.
Wm. Sprague,	John Nugent.
Fremont,	Oscar Healey.
Louis Osborn,	W. J. Flynn.

OFFICE, END OF T WHARF.

Vessels Towed

To and from all the Wharves in the City; through Bridges; to and from any of the Seaport Towns, and to New-York and the Vineyard. Vessels pumped out with a powerful steam pump. Casks filled with water for ballast, and vessels steamed and freed from vermin.

FRANK C. CATES, Asst. Manager.   **THOS. I. WINSOR,** Gen'l Manager.
GEORGE A. EATON, Soliciting Agent.

a.2

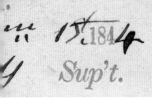

The Deck of the *Gitana*, 1883

Nathaniel L. Stebbins (1847–1922)

b

c

a.1

THE VIEW AFT ABOARD THE schooner-yacht *Gitana*, (left, bottom) swinging at her mooring off Hull, Massachusetts, then the center of Boston-area yachting. (*Gitana* would later follow the shift of yachting to Marblehead.) She was designed by the noted Boston naval architect D. J. Lawlor for William F. Weld, a grandson of the great Boston merchant and shipowner of the same name. The color postcard (left, top) depicts Hingham Bay and the Hull Yacht Club.

In the cabin, above, note the piano to starboard. *Gitana* was widely traveled, sailing often to the Caribbean and several times to the Mediterranean. When at sea, of course, carpets, clocks, tablecloths, spittoon, and other such fragile furnishings or potential projectiles would be safely stowed away.

Formalized American yachting began about 1800 in Boston and New York harbor waters. Many pioneering yachtsmen were members of wealthy shipping families, and their sloops and schooners were of fair size. *Gitana* represented a continuation of this tradition, although by this date the great Weld fleet had been all but liquidated and the assets shrewdly invested onshore.

TELEPHONE 1274
CORTLANDT

FRANKLIN SQ. L STATION
IS THE NEAREST

HOWARD PLACE
UNIFORM OUTFITTER

YACHT CREWS
UNIFORMED
According to Club Regulations

The correct shape of the different Yacht Club Caps in stock at all times

SAILOR PANTS, SHIRTS, CAPS, SHOES, NAVAL RESERVE UNIFORMS
ALWAYS ON HAND.

162 and 163 South St. (Corner Dover St.) New York
(170)

d

American.	Corinthian. N.Y.	Hull.	New York
Atlantic.	Corinthian. Marblehead.	Larchmont.	Portland
Beverly.	Corinthian, Hull.	Lynn.	Rhode Islan
Boston.	Dorchester.	Massachusetts.	Seawanhak
Bunker Hill.	Eastern.	New Bedford	South Bosto

The Start of the City Regatta, Boston Harbor, July 4, 1887

Nathaniel L. Stebbins (1847–1922)

1911

SLOOPS RACE ON A SPARKLING and glorious Fourth of July. The regatta sometimes attracted eighty or more entries.

By mid-century the sailing of small boats—mostly catboats—for pleasure and sport had become increasingly popular among a wide range of participants. The late nineteenth century saw a blossoming of activity, both in large and small craft, reflecting the great rise in the numbers of the middle class and the wealthy. Yacht clubs multiplied, and race results were front page news. The company that ran excursion steamers from Boston to Nantasket contributed prize money to encourage a large turnout of competitors, the better to attract more passengers.

U.S.S. *Wabash,* Boston Navy Yard, Charlestown, Massachusetts, 1890s

Photographer unknown

a

RECRUITS, AS AT A PICNIC, KNEEL around a mess cloth on the vast housed-over spar deck of the U.S.S. *Wabash.* (Meals were normally eaten below from tables hung from deck beams.) When new in 1854, the 2,918-ton steam screw frigate (right, center, shown after her lofty rig had been removed) was among the world's most powerful warships. Rendered obsolete by Civil War ironclads, she would remain on the Navy List into the early 1900s as a stationary "receiving" ship at Charlestown. Floating dormitories, receiving ships served as indoctrination stations for recruits and provided never-ending repair work for politically connected navy yard employees.

A sailor billeted aboard *Wabash* in 1886 described her spotless spar deck, swarming with raw recruits, as "an immense caravansary,—a warlike world by itself." Young Samuel Eliot Morison, the future historian and admiral, was taken aboard *Wabash* by his well-connected father and measured for a miniature sailor suit.

View from Bridge of the Battleship Minnesota

b

c

d

e

One of the Close Shaves of a Sailor's Life

A Liberty Party

f

The Mascot of the

g

U. S. BATTLESHIP "IOWA,"

THE
STROBRIDGE
LITHO · CO

1905

The Navy fits young America
for Peace and Progress

d

MARCH

SUN	MON	TUE	WED	THU	FRI	SAT
			1	2	3	4
5	6	7	8	9	10	11
12	13	14	15	16	17	18
19	20	21	22	23	24	25
26	27	28	29	30	31	

c

RIGHT 1898 BY KOE

Missouri, October 21, 1903

Nathaniel L. Stebbins (1847–1922)

a

THE NEW BATTLESHIP—she has not yet been commissioned as the U.S.S. *Missouri*—with hand-picked coal stokers, engineers, and helmsman, undergoing speed trials off Cape Ann. Her first run over the course had been below her contract speed of eighteen knots. The failure of a warship to meet the contract speed could lead to lengthy and costly alterations and litigation.

The second run was an all-out effort, with thick smoke, highlighted by occasional tongues of flame pouring from her stacks, that gave her Newport News, Virginia, builders a sixth-of-a knot cushion. The engineers were oil-soaked from the shower thrown off by her massive reciprocating engines. In the furnace compartments, the forty-eight hard-laboring stokers had to take care not to be drawn too close to the searing fires by the forced draft. Although reflective of the modernization of the turn of the century navy, *Missouri* would be rendered obsolete in but a few years by turbine-powered battleships of the Dreadnought type.

Brant Rock Beach, Marshfield, Massachusetts, mid-1890s

L. B. Howard (active early 1890s)

a

b

c

d

e

THE 4TH OF JULY.

SOUTH SHORE OF MASSACHUSETTS BAY

The New York New Haven and Hartford RAILROAD CO.

COASTAL RESORTS WERE important consumers of Maine lumber delivered by small schooners, and lumber for Brant Rock's buildings was unloaded at nearby Green Harbor.

Brant Rock's resort community dated from the 1870s. The ancient pattern of land division, which allotted upland farmers narrow strips of salt meadow that extended across the barrier beach, likely contributed to the congestion of the cottages. The great "Portland Gale" of November 1898 devastated this beach and its buildings, while at adjoining Ocean Bluff, only fifty of three-hundred cottages survived. In 1900, Brant Rock claimed four hotels and more than 320 cottages, with but twenty houses occupied by local fishermen.

Horse-drawn passenger "barges" connected with the railroad. Vendors of groceries and ice made their daily rounds. Gala celebrations were held on July 4th and Labor Day. This era ended with the Ocean Bluffs fire of April 1941, which burned two hotels, the post office, the casino, the church, twelve stores, 446 houses and cottages, ninety-six garages, and even fire engines. Smoke was seen from as far away as Nantucket. In the photograph, a Life-Saving Service crew drills near the 1893 station (with cupola).

Life-Savers, Orleans, Massachusetts, February 25, 1899

Photographer unknown

a.1

Rescued from the Wreck.

b

AT THE ORLEANS United States Life-Saving Service station—one of thirteen Cape Cod stations—surfmen launch their surfboat for a drill. Between 1875 and 1914, over six hundred vessels were lost on Cape Cod. The founder of the Life-Saving Service, Sumner Kimball, a Maine man, had once taught school at Orleans. In an era notorious for political graft, Kimball's creation of this effective and incorruptible agency in the 1870s was a notable achievement. Most wrecks occurred in winter storms—there were so few summertime casualties that stations were not even manned then—and surfmen often performed acts of remarkable endurance and heroism.

At right, the wreck of the iron bark *Frances*, of Hamburg. Wreckers are shown salvaging cargo—heavy tackles have been positioned over the holds. The wreckers' schooner floats inshore of the wreck. The badly iced-up bark was first driven onto the outer bar during a northeast gale on the night of December 26, 1872. The crew of fourteen was rescued while not far away the Boston ship *Peruvian* was lost with all hands on Peaked Hill Bar. Returning from the East Indies, *Peruvian* was carrying the crew of a wrecked Boston ship in addition to her own crew.

Frances, Truro, Massachusetts, 1873

George H. Nickerson (1835–1890)

a.2

c

d

f

e

DARRY THE LIFE SAVER

FRANK V. WEBSTER

---

194   HARPER'S NEW MONTHLY MAGAZINE.

"SITTING, STITCHING IN A MOURNFUL MUSE."

one would se
advantage.
when the f
full of pea-nu
and the air i
with smoke,
salamander
hot and s
with occasion
tions of t
juice, the lit
cle rises t
height of t
casion. Som
all talk at
"When I wa
Snow, in the
iant," one l
but some h
engine throw
off the trac
soon gets on
and begins
his story in a
key, only to b
suppressed.
have all he
scores and sc
times. He g
with a snort,
rest go on sp

pin. Twenty years ago there was a new de- | their yarns. Some of them have los
parture. The town had its ship-yard, and | ing by a hundred repetitions. If the

Porch-Sitting, the Chequesset Inn, Wellfleet, Massachusetts, 1913

The New England News Company (active c. 1905–1925)

a

BUILT IN 1902 BY CAPTAIN LORENZO BAKER, the hotel was the centerpiece of a luxury resort complex. Young Irish women from Boston composed
much of the staff. Guests traveled from Boston to Provincetown aboard steamers in which Captain Baker also had an interest. Baker, whose pioneering development of
the banana trade bore considerable fruit as the United Fruit Company, owned two hotels
at Port Antonio, Jamaica, for winter patronage.

Capitalizing on the unhealthful conditions of many cities and the suffering from
diseases little helped by medical science, resorts commonly promoted the healing prop-
erties of their pure air or medicinal waters. Many were cheaply banged-together fire-
traps, and in 1893, coinciding with worsening financial conditions, about twenty big
New England resort hotels conveniently vaporized. A higher-class establishment, the
Chequesset would die not by fire but by ice, which undercut the wharf pilings. The mam-
moth rockers—one is shown being operated by an elderly gentleman—were designed not
to take flight in a strong wind and are still sought after.

b

SWAMPSCOTT, MASS. NEW OCEAN HOUSE.

c

Colonial, Watch Hill, R. I.

Girl and Buoy on the Maine Coast.

d

e

8400

b

MINCED CODFISH.

HENRY MAYO & CO.
BOSTON.

c

Fishermen, Province
Mass. (First land
place of the Pilgri
Nov. 11, 1620. O.

d

Codfish Curing, Provincetown, Massachusetts, 1870s

George H. Nickerson (1835–1890) and William M. Smith (active 1870s–1880s)

12103—*Provincetown Harbor from Town Hill, Provincetown, Mass*

a

AFTER A VISIT IN 1849, HENRY DAVID THOREAU wrote, "A great many houses here were surrounded by fish-flakes close up to the sills on all sides . . . instead of looking out into a flower or grass plot, you looked on to so many square rods of cod turned wrong side outwards." After a later visit, he noted that the bedbugs and the sounds made by the cats that swarmed atop the town's roofs made sleep impossible.

In 1880, Provincetown fishermen were engaged in the offshore and 'longshore and winter cod fisheries, the mackerel fishery, the local gill-net fishery, the hake fishery, lobster trapping, and whaling. One-third of the six thousand inhabitants were "Portuguese," brought from the Azores (or, the "Western Islands") by whalers. In 1855, her whaling fleet numbered fifty-four vessels. In the 1870s, nearly eighty schooners manned by more than eight hundred men engaged in the mackerel fishery, and more than sixty schooners were employed in the Grand Banks cod fishery.

Blackfish, Probably on the Bay Side of Cape Cod, c. 1900

Photographer unknown

PRESUMABLY SINCE TIME IMMEMORIAL, BLACKFISH—not fish at all, but mammals—have beached themselves in treacherous, shoal Cape Cod Bay. Whereas today people try to save stranded blackfish, in times past, beginning with the Indians, people rushed out to drive the creatures to their doom. Thoreau wrote of thirty miles of Cape Cod beaches made unwalkable from the stench of the rotting remains of blackfish rendered for oil. A lighthouse keeper, upon finding a large stranded school one morning, cut his initials in each one and sold them for $1,000.

The mastless catboats, converted to power, date the photograph to the early 1900s. These may be Finnish quahogers from Wellfleet, who owned a fleet of such craft.

Old Windmill, West Falmouth, Massachusetts, c. 1890

Baldwin Coolidge (1845–1928)

b

c

WATCH FOR
DUTCHLANDS

DUTCHLAND
REG. U.S. PAT. OFF.
FARMS
ICE CREAM
EST.
1897
BROCKTON, MASS.
CLOSE COVER BEFORE STRIKING

WITHOUT STREAMS to power mills, Cape Codders employed the wind to grind grain (mostly corn) and also salt. Mills also pumped seawater for saltmakers. The West Falmouth mill (at right), built in 1787, was said to be able to grind seventy-five bushels of corn per day. It stood forty feet high with sails measuring fifty feet from tip to tip.

Henry David Thoreau, after his 1849 Cape Cod trip, wrote, "The most foreign and picturesque structures on the Cape, to an inlander, not excepting the salt-works, are the wind-mills— gray-looking, octagonal towers, with long timbers slanting to the ground in the rear, and there resting on a cart-wheel, by which their fans are turned round to face the wind. . . . A great circular rut was worn around the building by the wheel. The neighbors who assemble to turn the mill to the wind are likely to know which way it blows, without a weather-cock. They looked . . . like huge wounded birds, trailing a wing or a leg, and reminded one of pictures of the Netherlands."

Former sailors, adept at laying aloft, made good millers. Cape Cod's mills were moved about with some frequency; in 1922, the West Falmouth mill was moved to Brockton, Massachusetts, to serve as a trademark for an ice cream company. Two years later it joined the long list of venerable old structures to burn on a Halloween night.

Falmouth Heights, Massachusetts, c. 1910

The New England News Company (active c. 1905–1925)

b

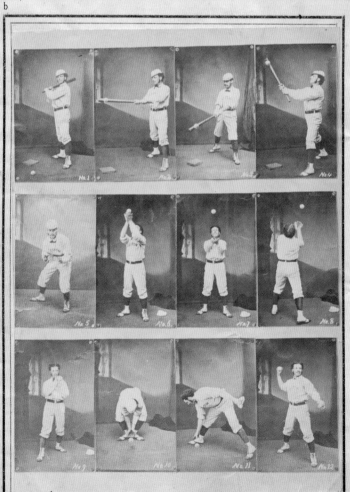

PICTURES BY SMITH & BOUSLEY, OF SALEM, MASS.

c

WRIGHT & DITSON
"HONOR MADE"
Athletic and Sports Goods

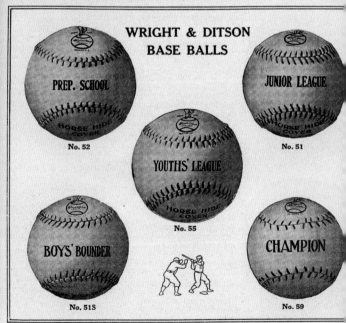

WRIGHT & DITSON
BASE BALLS

PREP. SCHOOL — HORSE HIDE COVER — No. 52

JUNIOR LEAGUE — HORSE HIDE COVER — No. 51

YOUTHS' LEAGUE — HORSE HIDE COVER — No. 55

BOYS' BOUNDER — No. 51S

CHAMPION — No. 59

No. 52. PREP SCHOOL LEAGUE. An excellent ball for amateur use. Durable materials are used in the construction. A well stitched, strong horsehide cover assures wear. Stitched with red and green thread. It is made in regulation size. Each, 50c.

No. 51. JUNIOR LEAGUE. This ball is made in Junior size and weight. It is the boys' favorite. Constructed of durable materials which assure good playing quality. Genuine horsehide cover. Stitched with red and green thread. An exceptionally lively ball. . . . . Each, 50c.

No. 51S. BOYS' BOUNDER. The Bounder is a boys' size, sturdily constr ball made to stand hard knocks. Has a genuine horsehide leather cover and is stitched with strong thread. . Each

No. 55. YOUTHS' LEAGUE. A ful ball made of good materials to stand use. Genuine horsehide leather cover, stitched with linen thread. The best size ball sold at the price. . Each

No. 59. CHAMPION. Boys' size. S waterproof, imitation leather cover, stitched with heavy thread. The best ball on the market. . . . . . Each

a.2

BALL GAME, FALMOUTH HEIGHTS, MASS.

d

e

WR...

WRIGH...

No. **PM.** WRIGHT & DITSON "PLAYERS" MODEL BATS. W...
Ditson "Players" Model Bats are made of the finest quality Northern
growth white ash. This timber is thoroughly air dried and seasoned, whic...
the fibre and produces the greatest driving power. There is no better woo...
purpose than the timber used in these bats. Each bat is double oil te...
boiling oil and hard filled and hand polished to a natural color, satin fin...
Any Mo...

Nine best models branded with the names of the following players:
Geo. Burns   "Pie" Traynor   Geo. Kelly   R. T. Peckinpaugh Fred...
Walter French   Duffy Lewis   C. L. Hartnett   Frank Schulte

ADAMS

WALKER

No. **150.** BAT. A high grade bat made of selected and thoroughly seasoned, second
growth white ash. Natural color with fine polished finish. Made in a selection of
the most popular models. Nicely balanced and proportioned to give the utmost
in driving power. . . . . Each, **$1.50**

Models branded with the names of the following players:
Earl "Sparky" Adams   Elliott   Curtis Walker

WE DO NOT GUARANTEE BATS

GHT & DITSON
"HONOR MADE"
Athletic and Sports Goods

CATCHERS' MASKS

No. **JP.** The frame is made of one
solid piece of light weight, special
composition metal, guaranteed to
withstand any shock or blow of...

No. RU

No. 400

No. 40S

No. **30S.** ASSOCIATION. Extra strength
steel wire. Welded joints. Open Vision
model. Fitted with removable sun shade. Adjustable pads and head straps. Each, **$4.00**

40S. LEAGUE. Strong steel wire.
Open Vision model. Has removable sun
hade. Leather pads and adjustable head
traps. . . . . Each, **$3.00**

No. **3M.** YOUTHS' MODEL. Black
enameled steel wire. Fitted with leather
face pads and adjustable head strap.
. . . . Each, **$2.00**

CM. BOYS' SPECIAL. Made of gun   No. **SS.** SUNSHADE. Of green material.

f

ONCE THE SITE OF a summer Indian encampment,
and later a sheep pasture, Falmouth Heights was developed by businessmen from Worcester, Massachusetts,
about 1870. Although their company failed in the Panic of 1873,
birds of a feather continued to flock together. Similar colonies
of well-off neighbors from hot, grimy inland towns occurred all
along the coast. In the early 1900s, other newcomers—"Portuguese" farmers—were turning inland Falmouth into one of the
country's leading strawberry growing regions.

On the ball field, the bases are loaded. The Falmouth Heights
diamond was considered the most pleasant venue in the famous
Cape Cod League, especially when an onshore breeze blew the
mosquitoes away and made home runs out of long flies. Hitting
the house in right field was scored a ground rule double. Shingle-
sheathed Queen Anne "cottages," like the one with the tower
looking out to the Sound, consumed much of Maine's vast shin-
gle production, said to be all sold east of the Connecticut River.

Augustus Hunt, Boston, late 1880s

Baldwin Coolidge (1845–1928)

THE HANDSOME BOW OF THE 1882 four-masted centerboard schooner *Augustus Hunt*, of Bath, Maine, with her carved billethead and trailboard. Deep-loaded with mid-Atlantic coal, the *Hunt* has made port against a bitter nor'west gale. The sailors are removing the remains of a blown-out jib—imagine the footing conditions out on the iced-up, plunging bowsprit when at sea! In 1886, sailors shipping on coasting schooners from Boston in the winter were receiving between fifteen and eighteen dollars per month, down from twenty in warm weather months, when demand was greater. Sooner or later schooners, and also barges, commonly came to a cold end—on January 22, 1904, the *Hunt* fatally stranded on Long Island, New York. Eight persons were lost, two were rescued.

Lightship in Ice, January 22, 1893

Nathaniel L. Stebbins (1847–1922)

a

THE VIEW ABOVE IS TAKEN FROM A STEAMER approaching the lightship, anchored in eastern Nantucket Sound between Monomoy Point, Cape Cod, and Great Point, Nantucket. The lightship is not moving; the floe ice is moving, carried by the tide. In 1874–75, the several Nantucket Sound lightships were swept from their stations by heavy ice floes.

Half a dozen or so lightships—and lighthouses as well—marked the perilous shipping paths through Vineyard and Nantucket sounds. By transiting the sounds, mariners avoided the often even more hazardous outside passage around Nantucket Shoals. In 1883, twenty thousand vessels passed by Nantucket Sound's Cross Rip lightship. Cape Cod and the shoals marked the historical natural division between the watery territories of New York and Boston.

b

Wreck of the Juniata at Cohasset, Mass. in the great storm Nov. 27. 1897.

PICTORIAL CHRONICLES OF THE MIGHTY DEEP

THE SEA, ITS SHIPS & SAILORS

d

Hotel Nantasket, with ice 25 feet high in front, Feb. 14. 1898.

How would you like to be there? N.F.W.

e

b

NEW ENGLAND GAS AND COKE COMPA[N]
EVERETT, MASS.

c

110

Tecumseh, **April 1, 1890**

Nathaniel L. Stebbins (1847–1922)

a

vi   GAYLOR'S SHIP-BUILDERS' AND OUTFITTERS' DIRECTORY,

RAWSON & HITTINGER,
Manufacturers of the Most Improved
HOISTING ENGINES,
FOR USE ABOARD SAILING VESSELS.

These engines are designed for loading and discharging cargoes, working whatloes, when hoisting and opening anchors, or warping ship, hoisting sails, setting up rigging, standing sails ship, pumps, washing decks, and extinguishing fires. These engines have an upright marine tubular boiler, which is so arranged that it may be thoroughly cleaned; the water will not require to be done often, unless it has constant to use salt water; they are fitted with a large copper coil condenser, compact the circulating pump of large capacity, to be used for working decks or in case of fire, from water tank to hold 350 gallons. The six horse power engine may be run with a waste of not more than three gallons of water per day; the iron tank holds sufficient fresh water to run the engine 10 days, of ten hours each; the boiler is so constructed that salt water may be used without injury to it; care being taken to blow off, so that no salt may accumulate on the boiler. This machine will condense 300 gallons of fresh water in 24 hours.

We build all sizes and descriptions of Hoisting, Portable, and Stationary Engines, and Steam Yachts, from 2/2 to 100 h. p. Cylinders 2 to 16 in. Cylinders, Boilers, Tools, and General Mill Work.

Works, 72 Main Street, Cambridgeport, Mass.

Warehouse, 28 Cortlandt Street, New-York.

d

TECUMSEH, A BIG CENTERBOARD SCHOONER (above), "flying light," heads back towards a mid-Atlantic coal port. The tiny figures of the helmsman and the mate, standing aft, put the schooner's large size in perspective. Coal was the principal coastwise cargo. Responding to growing industrialism, the post-Civil War Eastern seaboard coasting fleet was, by 1900, the largest and most efficient in the world. Between 1870 and about 1920, in addition to countless two-masters, 1,758 three-masted East Coast schooners, along with 459 four-masters, 56 five-masters, and 10 six-masters, were built. The ability of the big schooners to sail without ballast, and the use of steam hoisting engines to hoist sails and anchors, made them economically feasible.

The coal barge *General McClellan* is shown at far left. Built at Thomaston, Maine, as a full-rigged ship in 1862, the barge discharges coal at a Boston coal pocket. Many obsolete old square-riggers were cut down as coal barges, joining purpose-built barges behind powerful tugs.

THE CODFISHING SETTLEMENTS at Siasconset, Sachacha, and Weweeder were established in desperation by islanders during the American Revolution, when neutral Nantucket's huge whaling fleet was crushed between the warring forces. In the late 1800s, 'Sconset became a resort community favored by artistic elements. The village became a mix of new and rehabbed old cottages, many of them quaintly decorated with shipcarvings obtained from a New Bedford, Massachusetts, shipbreaker by the village's New York promoter.

The view by Baldwin Coolidge (top) shows Broadway, obviously the town's widest street, and the Henry Sherman Wyer photograph (bottom) depicts fish houses along 'Sconset Bank, with an ingenious horse-drawn beach vehicle, likely termed a dray. The apron of beach below the bank, shown on the next page, was known as Codfish Park and became a black community, its shacks occupied by domestics serving the tourists above.

CASTLE BANDBOX, 'SCONSE

Siasconset Village, Nantucket, Massachusetts, 1880s

Baldwin Coolidge (1845–1928) and Henry Sherman Wyer (1847–1920)

a.1

a.2

NTUCKET ISLAND, MASS.

Siasconset Village, Nantucket, Massachusetts, 1880s

Henry Sherman Wyer (1847–1920)

The Wreck of the *Wm. F. Marshall,* March 9, 1877

Josiah Freeman (1834–1902)

a

The Wreck of the *Wm. F. Marshall,* March 9, 1877

Josiah Freeman (1834–1902)

e Breeches Buoy in Action

c

ON THE SOUTH SIDE OF NANTUCKET, Massachusetts, heavy seas pound the bark *Wm. F. Marshall* of Saint John, New Brunswick. Built in 1876 at Bear River, Nova Scotia, the bark had been sailing in ballast from Hampton Roads, Virginia, to Saint John. She struck during a thick fog, and, until hailed by a life-saver from the beach, her people thought they were on an offshore shoal. Timely soundings presumably could have prevented the disaster. A "breeches buoy" apparatus with sling attached was made fast to the vessel, and the crew of fourteen, the wife and child of the steward, and a Newfoundland dog were brought safely ashore. Extensive preparations were made to refloat the bark, but heavy gales in July ended the effort. The bark was then burned to salvage metal.

Capitalizing on the decline of the American fleet, the "English"-flag deep-water fleets of Yarmouth, Nova Scotia, and Saint John, New Brunswick, flourished in the 1860s and '70s.

117

b

c

e

Thomas Sandsbury, Tuckernuck Island, Massachusetts, c. 1884

William Sturgis Bigelow (1850–1926)

TUCKERNUCK ISLANDERS WERE a tribe of lean opportunists, living by fishing, "market hunting" for seabirds, serving (and shaking down) wealthy bird hunters, and by "wrecking." Boston photographer and sport hunter Dr. William Sturgis Bigelow, a summer resident and a noted expert on Japanese culture, was regularly confounded in his dealings with the far more mysterious and inscrutable Tuckernuckers. He is shown at left in Japanese attire above a photograph of his cottage.

Tuckernuck, west of Nantucket and east of neighboring Muskeget Island, lay amidst some of the most perilous waters on the seaboard. Wreckers salvaged items of value from wrecked ships and also helped save imperiled ships, for pay. Islanders had long served as life-savers, and many found employment with the Life-Saving Service after its establishment. In an April 1879 storm, Thomas Sandsbury (shown above) commanded a crew of fellow Tuckernuck volunteers in the heroic rescue of several shipwrecked crews. All were awarded gold medals. In 1883, Sandsbury became the first keeper of the new Muskeget Station. He would later serve as the keeper of the Madaket Station, on Nantucket, one of four stations located in Nantucket County by 1892.

RICH'S GRILL

ESTABLISH
OCT. 14.

155 FEDERAL ST.
NEAR SOUTH TERMINAL

GAME
and
SEA FOOD
for
Connoisseurs

WHAT WE SERVED IN THE LINE OF GAME
DURING THE SEASON OF 1907-1908

Moose	1	Guinea Hens	206
Black Bear	4	Beatle Head	26
Deer	6	Canvas Backs	326
Coons	9	Red Heads	303
Possum	2	Mallards	454
Grey Squirrels	26	Blacks	374
German Hares	136	Widgeon	192
Wild Swan	75	Frant	199
Wild Geese	688	Butter Balls	263
Pheasants	6	Teal	51
French Partridge	39	Grass Birds	120
English Grouse	31	Rail Birds	9
Quail	326	Doe Birds	9
Golden Plover	184	Coot	1022

Oak Bluffs, Martha's Vineyard, Massachusetts, 1905 or later

Thomson and Thomson (active c. 1905–1915)

a

c

No. 229. Clinton Av., from Spinney's Camp Ground.

b

d

e

R. UNCATENA, OAK BLUFFS, MASS.

f

SWIMMERS AT OAK BUFFS, having disrobed and then rerobed themselves in the bathhouses, descend staircases like lemmings. At resorts, the wearing of even neck-to-knee bathing attire anywhere other than on the beach was unacceptable—indeed, clothing which even revealed females to be bipeds offended some sensibilities. Here, the very beach has been sacrificed for the sake of public propriety (and private profit).

The town broke off from Edgartown in 1880; first called "Cottage City," it became Oak Bluffs in 1907. Beginning in the 1830s, an oak grove had been the site of an annual Methodist prayer meeting. After the Civil War, coastal "camp meetings"—which permitted the pious to recreate without guilt—flourished. At Oak Buffs, as elsewhere, closely grouped tents were replaced by tiny gingerbread cottages. Fed by steamers, the town evolved into a teeming summer resort for members of the general public. The Methodists, in response, walled-off the campground with a seven-foot picket fence, accessed through a gate that was locked at ten p.m.

Gay Head Light, Martha's Vineyard, Massachusetts, 1887

Baldwin Coolidge (1845–1928)

a.1

ALDWIN COOLIDGE Phot. BOSTON Nº 2109

THE LIGHTHOUSE (ABOVE) stands atop a cliff at the island's western end. The "Indian omnibus" hauled visitors up from the wharf served by steamers from Cottage City. The tower as shown had last been rebuilt in the 1850s. The first tower was built in 1799; its keeper, Ebenezer Skiff, complained that he had to import his firewood from the mainland, since the local Wampanoag Indians beat him to any driftwood. The wind vane is of a sperm whale, reminding us that the Indians gained fame as harpooners in the whale fishery. After the terrible wreck of the steamer *City of Columbus* in December, 1884, Indian life-savers (right, bottom) received gold medals for their selfless bravery.

The cedars (right, above), said to be capable of supporting a person walking atop them, were another favored site, especially for picnicking.

Gay Head's multicolored cliffs (following page) were a major destination for early tourists, who faced a dusty, tedious two-day round-trip through thirty or so farmers' gates and barways if they decided to come by land from Edgartown.

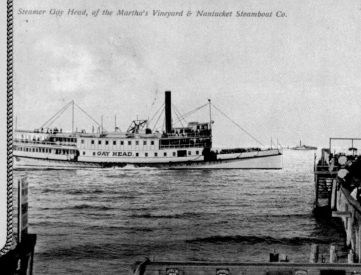

Steamer Gay Head, of the Martha's Vineyard & Nantucket Steamboat Co.

b

c

Gay Head, Martha's Vineyard, Massachusetts, 1894

Baldwin Coolidge (1845–1928)

a

b

GAY HEAD CLIFFS, MARTHA'S VINEYARD, MASS.

Captain and Mrs. Obed Delano, Marion, Massachusetts, c. 1890

Photographer unknown

a

b

MAINTAINING A PROPER FENCE was an obligation taken to heart by all self-respecting Marioners. Delano had been a whaler, a Forty-Niner, a whaling captain, and owner of a whaling brig. As was traditional for retired captains, of which Marion had a surplus, Delano busied himself with public affairs, serving in the legislature, as selectman, moderator, justice of the peace, guardian of widows and orphans, and so on. When President and Mrs. Cleveland, vacationing in 1887, received the town, it was reported that "Capt. Obed Delano was busy keeping the line in motion."

Alexandrina Petrovna Kuzmishchova, the accomplished daughter of a Russian admiral, married the Delanos' son George. They met at St. Petersburg, when George was an ensign. "Aline's" piano, gold and silver service, icons, paintings, and such, were added to the house's trove of seagoing treasures. Her work as a translator would later pay the bills for George's failures in business.

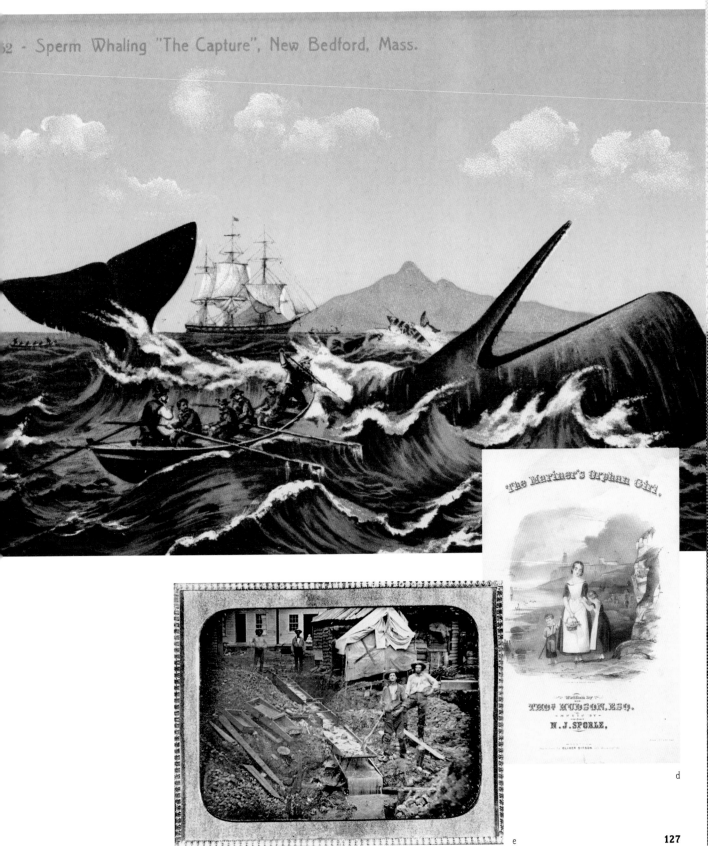

52 - Sperm Whaling "The Capture", New Bedford, Mass.

b

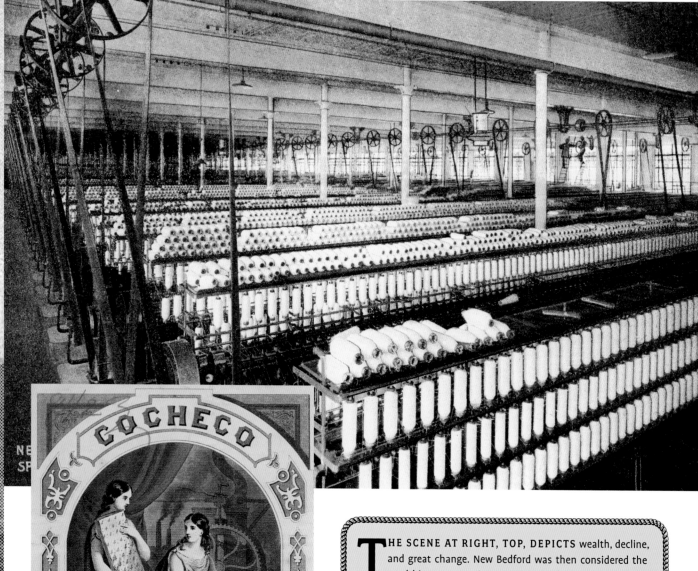

NE
SP

COCHECO

LAWRENCE & CO. BOSTON.

c

THE SCENE AT RIGHT, TOP, DEPICTS wealth, decline, and great change. New Bedford was then considered the wealthiest community per capita in the nation, although the source of its riches—whaling—was in steep decline. However, old money was busy making new, invested in miles of cotton mills at New Bedford and Fall River.

The bark, despite the whaleboat hung from whale-ship-style "cranes," is not a whaler but likely a "Western Isles," or, Azores, packet. Packets carried supplies for whalers out to the islands, returning with wine, oil, pottery, and people. The dried seaweed on the wharf protects casks of whale oil, vainly awaiting a rise in price. The granite building at right, built in the 1830s, long housed the counting house of leading whale ship owner Jonathan Bourne, Jr. A sailmaker occupied the post-less loft; sails were lowered down to waiting wagons tightly coiled in water and rat-resistant casks. Happily, the building still stands, if a bit bewildered by the changed world around it.

G 21734   Casks of Whale Oil, awaiting a market, New Bedford, Mass.

d

b

Employe's Ticket

Launching of cup defender "Reliance"

Saturday, April the eleventh

nineteen hundred and three

five-thirty P. M.

Pass Mr. .... *with lady*

to North Wharf   *Herreshoff Mfg. Co.*

THE AMERICA'S CUP DEFENDER *Reliance* smokes past the Brenton Reef light vessel in a pre-trials race. *Reliance* was the biggest of all the Cup yachts. Designed by builder Nat Herreshoff to take advantage of a measurement rule, *Reliance*'s long overhangs increased the effective waterline length but did not result in a wholesome, seaworthy design. *Reliance* was an engineering marvel. The bronze hull, measuring 144 feet on deck, was longitudinally framed. Her rig was over two hundred feet in length; her measured sail area was 16,200 square feet, all hung from a single, remarkably engineered mast. The topmast is housed inside the lower mast, its heel coming to rest just below the waterline. The hollow rudder was trimmed with water ballast. Advanced two-speed winches with disc clutches were mounted below deck. Yet, she was intended for but a single summer's sport.

Reliance is shown sailing right on the edge of her full sail-carrying ability. Another contender, *Constitution*, lost her topmast in this same race, while, later in the day, *Reliance*'s steel gaff collapsed. The gaff was seventy feet long—the length of the main boom of a good-sized, heavily canvassed Gloucester fishing schooner.

c

THE *AMERICA'S*
CUP RACES

BY HERBERT L. STONE

d

Olive E, August 9, 1906

Nathaniel L. Stebbins (1847–1922)

a

CATFISH.

WHITEFISH

SWORDFISH.

FLOUNDER.

THE NOANK, CONNECTICUT-BUILT SLOOP of Newport, Rhode Island, is fish-ting for swordfish. Noank was long noted for its stylish sloops and small schooners, many of which carried fish alive in a flooded "well" to the New York market.

The sloop looks to be well freighted with ice or ice and fish. Swordfish, when spotted on the surface, were harpooned from the pulpit. The dart of the harpoon was attached by a line to a keg; the keg was retrieved and the fish killed and boated from the dory now towing astern.

Twenty years before this photograph was taken, the public would not eat swordfish. Today, swordfish are found only far offshore, greatly reduced in numbers and in average size.

The *Olive E* had had a gasoline engine installed several years earlier. Although often accused of conservatism, few groups in society more quickly adopted the internal com-bustion engine than did fishermen.

Mystic, Connecticut, 1890s

Photographer unknown

a

b

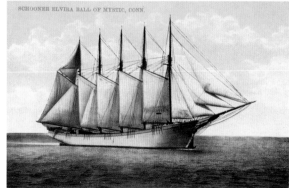

SCHOONER ELVIRA BALL OF MYSTIC, CONN.

c

A SMALL EXCURSION STEAMER, whose identity has escaped detection, boards passengers on the Mystic River. Young women are fashionably—if impractically, in a coal-burning age—dressed in white. The canopy shields white dresses from soot and desirably pallid complexions from sun.

Mystic had been a great shipbuilding town—in the cove beyond, masts and spars-to-be once floated in wet storage. Clipper ships and Civil War-era steamers had been the town's specialties. In the 1890s, the industry was moribund, although there would be a brief revival in the early 1900s, including the construction of a four- and a five-masted schooner just north of where the steamer is berthed. The top of the steeple of the Union Baptist Church and the steamer's stack vanished during the exposure.

Mystic's principal maritime occupation in the 1890s was the menhaden, or pogy, fishery. (Many Mainers manned the Mystic pogy steamers.) The pogy is an industrial fish, rendered for oil and fertilizer. Foul-smelling factories were located upwind of the village, and excursion steamers mercifully offered escape to New London's beaches, or to the resorts of Fishers Island, New York, or Watch Hill, Rhode Island. The pogy fleet followed the fish alongshore. A windy day made the schools invisible, sending the fleet into port, as shown in the accompanying view of Bridgeport, with local oyster sloops moored across the channel.

Priscilla Interior, 1920s (?)

William King Covell (1904 – 1975)

Fall River Line

Steamer PROVIDENCE

WEEK ENDING,
FEB. 22o, 1890.

Programme of Concerts

BY

HOOPER'S ORCHESTRA,

CHAS. E. HOOPER, Conductor.

Mr. J. I. PIETRES,　.　.　.　Violinist.

SOLOISTS:

Mr. URIAH HOWARD,　　　Mr. T. F. LYONS,
Mr. J. I. PIETRES.

AFTERNOON CONCERT FROM NEW YORK.

FROM 4 TO 6 P. M.

1 MARCH "Jube...
2 SCHOTTISCHE...
3 MEDLEY OVE...
4 CONCERT WA...
5 CONCERT POL...

6 MARCH "Expo...
7 NEWPORT "L...
8 SELECTION...
　　From Sulli...
9 CONCERT WA...
10 GALOP "Herm...

EVENING CO...

FRO...

1 MARCH "Carn...
2 OVERTURE "...
3 SOLO for CLA...

4 SELECTION "...
5 ROMANZA "A...

6 OVERTURE "...
7 GAVOTTE "H...
8 FINALE From the Opera, 'The Martyrs." ....Donizetti
9 CONCERT WALTZ "Ange d'Amour," ....Waldteufel
10 FINALE "...

TERWILLIGER & PECK...

b

Priscilla, August 21, 1896

Nathaniel L. Stebbins (1847–1922)

c

a.2

A VISITING SCOTSMAN called the *Priscilla*, "the most astonishing thing I have yet seen in this big country . . . . You go up a huge great staircase and find yourself in a concert hall. . . . You go up another magnificent staircase, and you lose yourself in hundreds of yards of lordly corridor. . . . you laugh at the ridiculous Aladdin who made his genie build such a city of a vessel under the impression that it is in the power of any machinery made by man to make the 'derned' thing move. . . . and before you know it you are doing three and twenty miles an hour." The Aladdin who designed and built the *Priscilla* was George Peirce, a native of Hallowell, Maine. Frank Hill Smith designed the Italian Renaissance interior. Above, *Priscilla* departs New York for Fall River, Massachusetts, where she will connect with the Boston train. She carried up to fifteen hundred passengers with a crew of two hundred.

Fall River Line
Established 1847

Daily Service
All Year Round
New York and Boston
and New England Points
The New England Steamship Company

d

a.1

ILLUSTRATION SOURCES
AND BIBLIOGRAPHY

Page numbers are printed in bold-
face. All of the images are from
the collection of Historic New
England unless otherwise noted.

Frontispiece. Marine view from Oak Bluffs, Martha's Vineyard, Massachusetts, c. 1870. Photographer unknown.

10: Detail of postcard of clam diggers, Provincetown, Massachusetts, 1915 or earlier. *The Advocate*, publisher.

12–13: Lobster Canning Factory, Mount Desert, Maine, c. 1870
MAIN IMAGE:
a. E. L. Allen (active 1860s–1890s), photographer.
ADDITIONAL IMAGES:
b. Cover of *The Lobster Catchers* by James Otis. (New York: E. P. Dutton & Company, 1900.) Private Collection.
c. Advertising poster for Winslow's Green Corn and Globe Lobsters packed by the Portland Packing Company, Portland, Maine. Courtesy Maine Historic Preservation Commission.
d. Packaging label for the Castine Packing Co., Castine, Maine. Courtesy Wilson Museum, Castine, Maine.
e. Postcard of Mt. Katahdin from Kidney Pond, Maine. C. T. American Art, publisher. Courtesy Maine Historic Preservation Commission.
PRINCIPAL RESOURCES:
Bunting, W. H., compiler and editor.
  A Day's Work: A Sampler of Historic Maine Photographs, 1860–1920. Gardiner, Maine: Tilbury House; Portland, Maine: Maine Preservation, 1997: 228.
Martin, Kenneth R. and Nathan R. Lipfert. *Lobstering and the Maine Coast*. Bath, Maine: Bath Maritime Museum, 1985: 30–47.

14–15: Castine Ferry, Bagaduce River, Hancock County, Maine, c. 1896
MAIN IMAGE:
A. H. Folsom (active 1860s–1900s), photographer.
PRINCIPAL RESOURCES:
Bangor Daily News, March 23, 1938.
[Bangor] *Industrial Journal*, August 22, 1884.

16–17: Cobbler, Isle Au Haut, Eastern Penobscot Bay, Maine, c. 1896
MAIN IMAGE:
a. S. I. Carpenter (dates unknown), photographer.
ADDITIONAL IMAGES:
b. Stereo view of a shoemaker c. 1876. J. W. & J. S. Moulton, Salem, Massachusetts, photographers.
c. Illustration from the Spring and Summer product catalogue of The Stetson Shoe Company, Weymouth, Massachusetts, 1908.
d. Postcard of the Burgess and Lang Buildings, Haverhill, Massachusetts, c. 1914. M. Schlafman, publisher.
e. Stereo view of a shoe worker at a lasting machine, Lynn, Massachusetts. The Keystone View Company, publisher.
f. Advertising pamphlet for The Goodyear Boot & Shoe Sewing Machines, c. 1882.
PRINCIPAL RESOURCES:
Bunting, W. H., compiler and editor.
  A Day's Work: A Sampler of Historic Maine Photographs, 1860–1920. Gardiner, Maine: Tilbury House; Portland, Maine: Maine Preservation, 1997: 284.

18–19: Camden, Maine, c. 1900
MAIN IMAGE:
a. Photographer unknown.
ADDITIONAL IMAGES:
b. Postcard of Main Street, Camden, Maine, c. 1906. Hugh C. Leighton, Co., publisher. Courtesy Maine Historic Preservation Commission.
c. Postcard of Camden from Mountain. Hugh C. Leighton, Co., publisher. Courtesy Maine Historic Preservation Commission.
d. Postcard of Norumbega, Camden, Maine. G. W. Morris, publisher. Courtesy Maine Historic Preservation Commission.
e. Photograph of Knowlton Brothers Foundry, Camden, Maine. Photographer unknown. Courtesy Maine Historic Preservation Commission.
PRINCIPAL RESOURCES:
[Bangor] *Industrial Journal*, May 2, 1884;
  March 10, 1893; and September 7, 1900.

20–21: *Hotspur, 1885*
MAIN IMAGE:
a. Nathaniel L. Stebbins (1847–1922), photographer.
ADDITIONAL IMAGES:
b. Postcard of the launch of a "six master," Bath, Maine, 1913 or earlier. Hugh C. Leighton Co., publisher.
c. Photograph of a shipyard launching. Photographer unknown.
d. Stereo view of a man hand-finishing spars in a Rockland, Maine, shipyard. Underwood & Underwood, photographers.
PRINCIPAL RESOURCES:
Bunting, W. H. *Sea Struck*. Edgartown, Massachusetts: Martha's Vineyard Historical Society; New Bedford, Massachusetts: New Bedford Whaling Museum; Gardiner, Maine: Tilbury House, Publishers, 2004.
Lipfert, Nathan R. "Dangerous Statistics." *The Rhumb Line* (Summer 2003).

22–23: Biddeford Pool, Maine, c. 1880
MAIN IMAGE:
Baldwin Coolidge (1845–1928), photographer.
PRINCIPAL RESOURCES:
Smith, Joseph W. *Gleanings from the Sea: Showing the Pleasures, Pains and Penalties of Life Afloat with Contingencies Ashore*. Andover, Massachusetts: The Author, 1887.

24–25: George H. Donnell, York, Maine, early 1880s
MAIN IMAGE:
a. Emma L. Coleman (1853–1942), photographer.
ADDITIONAL IMAGES:
b. Page of advertisements from *The Boston Directory*. (Boston: Samson, Murdock, and Co., 1888.)
c. Postcard of a Cape Ann fisherman, 1905. Detroit Photographic Co., publisher.
d. Postcard of Cape Ann fisherman and dory, 1905. Detroit Photographic Co., publisher.

PRINCIPAL RESOURCES:
Goode, George B. *The Fisheries and Fishery Industries of the United States.* Washington: Government Printing Office, 1884–1887: Sec. IV, 11–13.

26–27: Clamming, York River, Maine, c. 1890
MAIN IMAGE:
a. Fred Quimby (1862–1896), photographer.
ADDITIONAL IMAGES:
b. Packaging label for Castine Bay Co. clams. Courtesy of Wilson Museum, Castine, Maine.
c. Photograph of family eating clams, Duxbury, Massachusetts. Photographer unknown.
d. Stereo view of a New England Clam Bake, c. 1870. Kilburn Brothers, photographers.
e. Trade card for the Arlington House "Rhode Island Clam Bake," Strawberry Hill, Rhode Island.
PRINCIPAL RESOURCES:
Bunting, W. H., compiler and editor. *A Day's Work: A Sampler of Historic Maine Photographs, 1860–1920.* Gardiner, Maine: Tilbury House; Portland, Maine: Maine Preservation, 1997: 162.

28–29: Farmer Loading his Cart with Kelp, Long Sands, York, Maine, 1882
MAIN IMAGE:
a. Emma L. Coleman (1853–1942), photographer.
ADDITIONAL IMAGES:
b. Postcard of Promenade Walk, York Beach, Maine. Thomson & Thomson, publishers.
c. Postcard of York Beach and Union Bluffs, York Beach, Maine, c. 1908. Hugh C. Leighton Co., publisher.
d. Postcard of Hotel Albracca, York, Maine. Hugh C. Leighton, Co., publisher. Courtesy Maine Historic Preservation Commission.
PRINCIPAL RESOURCES:
Bunting, W. H., compiler and editor. *A Day's Work: A Sampler of Historic Maine Photographs, 1860–1920.* Gardiner, Maine: Tilbury House; Portland, Maine: Maine Preservation, 1997: 124.
Thoreau, Henry David. *Cape Cod.* New York: Norton, 1951: 14.

30–31: Salt-Marsh Haying, Hampton, New Hampshire, c. 1890 / Gundalow *Fanny M,* Dover, New Hampshire, November 27, 1896
MAIN IMAGES:
a.1. C. M. Turner (dates unknown), photographer.
a.2. Nathaniel L. Stebbins (1847–1922), photographer.

ADDITIONAL IMAGES:
b. Postcard of the marshes, Plum Island, Newburyport, Massachusetts. Frank W. Swallow, Inc., publisher.
c. Postcard of salt haying, Polpis, Nantucket, Massachusetts, 1907 or earlier. Henry S. Wyer, publisher.
PRINCIPAL RESOURCES:
Bunting, W. H., compiler and editor. *A Day's Work: A Sampler of Historic Maine Photographs, 1860–1920.* Gardiner, Maine: Tilbury House; Portland, Maine: Maine Preservation, 2000: 176.
Taylor, D. Foster. "The Gundalow *Fanny M.*" *The American Neptune* (July 1942).

32–33: Portsmouth, New Hampshire, c. 1907
MAIN IMAGE:
a. Henry G. Peabody (1855–1951), photographer.
ADDITIONAL IMAGES:
b. Postcard of coal wharves, Portsmouth, New Hampshire, c. 1909. Detroit Publishing Co., publisher.
c. Postcard of the five-masted schooner *Paul Palmer,* Portsmouth, New Hampshire, 1908. Detroit Publishing Co., publisher.
d. Photographer's logo for Henry G. Peabody, Publisher of Photographic Views, Boston, c. 1892.
PRINCIPAL RESOURCES:
Candee, Richard M. *Atlantic Heights, A World War I Shipbuilders' Community.* Portsmouth, New Hampshire: Printed for the Portsmouth Marine Society by P. E. Randall, 1985: 13–20.
With thanks to: John Mayer, Maine Historical Society, and Richard E. Winslow III, volunteer, Portsmouth Public Library.

34–35: White Island Light, Isles of Shoals, New Hampshire, c. 1905
MAIN IMAGE:
a. Henry G. Peabody (1855–1951), photographer.
ADDITIONAL IMAGES:
b. Page from *My Lighthouse, and Other Poems,* by Celia Thaxter. (L. Prang & Company, 1890.) Courtesy Vaughn Cottage Memorial Library and Museum, Star Island Corporation.
c. Cover of *An Island Garden* by Celia Thaxter. (Boston and New York: Houghton, Mifflin & Co., 1894.)
d. Painting *In the Garden (Celia Thaxter in Her Garden),* 1892, by Childe Hassam. Courtesy Smithsonian American Art Museum, Washington, D. C.

PRINCIPAL RESOURCES:
Willoughby, Malcolm F. *Lighthouses of New England.* Boston: Metcalf, 1920: 127–29.

36–37: Salisbury Beach, Massachusetts, 1919
MAIN IMAGE:
a. The New England News Company (active c. 1905–1925), photographer.
ADDITIONAL IMAGES:
b. Panoramic postcard of Salisbury Beach, Massachusetts, c. 1920. J. S. Willow[?], publisher.
c. Souvenir program for "Wonderland," Revere Beach, Massachusetts, 1908. The Waters Press, publisher.
d. Brochure for the Nantasket Beach Steamboat Co., 1916.
e. Postcard of "Shooting the Chutes" at Wonderland, Revere Beach, Massachusetts, 1907. M. I. Robbins, publisher.
PRINCIPAL RESOURCES:
With thanks to: Alan MacInnes.

38–39: Postcard of Paragon Park, Nantasket Beach, Massachusetts, c. 1906. Metropolitan News Co., publisher.

40–41: Fish Market, Newburyport, Massachusetts, c. 1870
MAIN IMAGE:
a. H. P. Macintosh (1830–1907), photographer.
ADDITIONAL IMAGES:
b. Illustration of fish knife and fork from the trade catalogue, *The Colonial Book of The Towle Mfg. Company Silversmiths,* 1908. Courtesy Lorna Condon.
c. Stereo view of the Stocker-Wheelwright House, Newburyport, Massachusetts. Photographer unknown.
d. Photograph of the launching of the *Edith H. Symington,* George E. Currier Shipyard, Newburyport, Massachusetts. Photographer unknown.
e. Postcard of clam diggers and their shanties, "Joppa," Newburyport, Massachusetts, 1905. The Rotograph Co., publisher.
PRINCIPAL RESOURCES:
Cheney, Robert K. *Maritime History of the Merrimac & Shipbuilding.* Newburyport, Massachusetts: Newburyport Press, 1964.
Coffin, Edward M. *Merrimac River Shipping.* Newburyport, Massachusetts: The Historical Society of Old Newbury, 1926.

42–43: Plum Island, Newburyport, Massachusetts, c. 1905
MAIN IMAGE:
a. Thomson and Thomson (active c. 1905–1915), photographers.

ADDITIONAL IMAGES:
b. Map showing territory covered by the Bay State Street Railway Co., 1912.
c. Photograph of trolley in front of Plum Island Hotel, Newburyport, Massachusetts. Photographer unknown.
d. Brochure for the Bay State Street Railway Co., 1912.

44–45: *Nellie Moody,* **Gloucester, Massachusetts, c. 1890**
MAIN IMAGE:
a. Photographer unknown.
ADDITIONAL IMAGES:
b. Bill head for Harvey C. Smith, Wholesale Fish Dealer, Gloucester, Massachusetts, 1902.
c. Postcard of unloading Gorton's codfish, Gloucester, Massachusetts, 1905. Detroit Publishing Co., publisher.
d. Cover of promotional recipe book for preparing seafood. Frank E. Davis Co., publisher.
PRINCIPAL RESOURCES:
Goode, George B. *The Fisheries and Fishery Industries of the United States.* Washington: Government Printing Office, 1884–1887: Sec. II, 168.

46–47: Curtis Boys, Manchester, Massachusetts, 1880s
MAIN IMAGE:
a. Harriot Appleton Curtis (1841–1923), photographer.
ADDITIONAL IMAGES:
b. Advertisement for children's clothing, Terry & Cook, Agents, Boston, c. 1887.
c. Engraving from the book *The Nursery.* (Boston: The Nursery Publishing Co., 1880.)
d. Cover of *The Boy Mechanic.* (Chicago: Popular Mechanics Press, 1913.) Private Collection.
PRINCIPAL RESOURCES:
Halsted, Isabella. *The Aunts.* Manchester, Massachusetts: Sharksmouth Press, 1992.
Morison, Samuel Eliot. *The Maritime History of Massachusetts, 1780–1860.* Boston and New York: Houghton Mifflin, 1921: 245.

48–49: Figurehead, Peach's Point, Marblehead, Massachusetts, c. 1915
MAIN IMAGE:
a. Mary H. Northend (1850–1926), photographer.
ADDITIONAL IMAGES:
b. Sketch of sailboats by Robert Swain Peabody from his scrapbook/guestbook, 1897–1903.
c. Postcard of the Custom House, Boston. Mason Bros. & Co., publisher.
d. Photograph of the Boston Custom

House, 1913 or earlier. The Halliday Historic Photograph Co., photographer.
PRINCIPAL RESOURCES:
International Studio, September–October, 1922.
Peabody, Robert Swain. *An Architect's Sketch Book.* Boston and New York: Houghton Mifflin, 1912: 123.

50–51: The Racing Catboat *Koorali,* **June 17, 1892**
MAIN IMAGE:
a. Nathaniel L. Stebbins (1847–1922), photographer.
ADDITIONAL IMAGES:
b. Business card for N. L. Stebbins, commercial photographer.
c. Partial list of 8 x 10 N. L. Stebbins's photographs available for sale.
d. Photograph of Capt. N. L. Stebbins. Photographer unknown.
e. Cover of *The Yachtsman's Album.* (Boston: N. L. Stebbins, 1896.)
f. Cover of *The Illustrated Coast Pilot.* (Boston: N. L. Stebbins, 1896.)
PRINCIPAL RESOURCES:
Thompson, Winfield M. "Cats in Massachusetts Bay." *The Rudder* (July–August, 1908).

52–53: *Constellation,* **June 27, 1901**
MAIN IMAGE:
Nathaniel L. Stebbins (1847–1922), photographer.
PRINCIPAL RESOURCES:
Crowninshield, B. B. *Fore-and-Afters.* Boston and New York: Houghton Mifflin, 1940: 87–88.

54–55: *Turtle,* **August 11, 1912**
MAIN IMAGE:
a. Nathaniel L. Stebbins (1847–1922), photographer.
ADDITIONAL IMAGES:
b, e. Pages from the engineer's notebook, 1903, for the steamer *Turtle.*
c. Deck and shear plan for the steamer *Turtle,* 1903, by F. H. Walker.
d. "Str. Turtle" stamp from the engineer's notebook, 1903, for the steamer *Turtle.*
PRINCIPAL RESOURCES:
With thanks to: Paul Stubing.

56–57: A Swampscott Dory, Swampscott, Massachusetts, c. 1890
MAIN IMAGE:
a. Charles P. Jeffers and Wardwell (active late 1880s), photographers.
ADDITIONAL IMAGES:
b. Trade card for R. T. Dodge & Co., Boston.
c. Bill head for E. Gerry Emmons, Swampscott, Massachusetts, 1894.

d. Swampscott dory, Swampscott, Massachusetts, c. 1900. Stuart P. Ellis, photographer.
e. Postcard of Fisherman's Beach, Swampscott, Massachusetts, 1907 or earlier. The New England News Company, publisher.
f. Program for Dory Regatta, Swampscott, Massachusetts, August 27, 1859.
PRINCIPAL RESOURCES:
Boston Journal, January 7, 1878.
Bunting, W. H., compiler and editor. *A Day's Work: A Sampler of Historic Maine Photographs, 1860–1920.* Gardiner, Maine: Tilbury House; Portland, Maine: Maine Preservation, 1997: 176.
Smith, Joseph W. *Gleanings from the Sea: Showing the Pleasures, Pains and Penalties of Life Afloat with Contingencies Ashore.* Andover, Massachusetts: The Author, 1887: 228.

58–59: *Panay,* **June 6, 1887**
MAIN IMAGE:
a. Nathaniel L. Stebbins (1847–1922), photographer. Courtesy W. H. Bunting.
ADDITIONAL IMAGES:
b. Advertisement for S. Thaxter and Son Nautical and Yachting Instruments, Boston. Courtesy W. H. Bunting.
c. "Interior of Ropewalk, Plymouth Cordage Company," from *The Story of Rope: The History and the Modern Development of Rope-Making.* (North Plymouth, Massachusetts: Plymouth Cordage Company, 1925, p. 82.)
d. Detail of a lithograph depicting the Sewall, Day & Co.'s Cordage Manufactory, Boston. Drawn from nature and lithographed by J. P. Newell. Printed by J. H. Bufford.
PRINCIPAL RESOURCES:
Bunting, W. H., compiler and annotator. *Portrait of a Port: Boston, 1852–1914.* Cambridge, Massachusetts: Harvard University Press, 1971: 346, 348.

60–61: *Independence,* **1884**
MAIN IMAGE:
a. Nathaniel L. Stebbins (1847–1922), photographer.
ADDITIONAL IMAGES:
b. Cargo book of the ship *Agnes.*
c. Ship sailing card for the Henry W. Peabody & Co. Australian Line, Boston.
PRINCIPAL RESOURCES:
Eustis, Frederic A. *Augustus Hemenway, 1805–1876, Builder of the United States Trade with the West Coast of South America.* Salem, Massachusetts: Peabody Museum, 1955.

62–63: *Hesper* / **Marine Railway**
MAIN IMAGES:
a.1. Nathaniel L. Stebbins (1847–1922), photographer.
a.2. Photographer unknown.
ADDITIONAL IMAGES:
b. Advertisement for Providence Dry Dock and Marine Railway Co., from *Eldridge's Coast Pilot No. 4.* (Boston: Geo. W. Eldridge, 1893.) Courtesy W. H. Bunting.
c. Trade card for the D. D. Kelly marine railway, East Boston.
d. Postcard of Dry Dock, Portsmouth Navy Yard, Portsmouth, New Hampshire, 1908. Detroit Publishing Co., publisher.
PRINCIPAL RESOURCES:
Eastman, Ralph Mason. *Pilots and Pilot Boats of Boston Harbor.* Boston: Privately printed for the Second Bank-State Street Trust Co., 1956: 48–49.
Republican Journal, October 2, 1884.

64–65: **Pilot Schooner** *Varuna*, **Boston, 1890s**
MAIN IMAGE:
a. Photographer unknown.
ADDITIONAL IMAGES:
Background. Bird's Eye View of Boston Harbor and South Shore to Provincetown Showing Steamboat Routes, c. 1907. John F. Murphy, publisher.
PRINCIPAL RESOURCES:
Erkkila, Barbara H. *Hammers on Stone: A History of Cape Ann Granite.* Woolwich, Maine: TBW Books, 1980: 27.
Hauk, Zarah William. *The Stone Sloops of Chebeague and the Men Who Sailed Them; Also Some Chebeague Miscellany.* Boston: [n.p.] 1949: 17.
Lampee, Charles I. "Memories of Cruises on Boston Pilot Boats of Long Ago." *Nautical Research Journal*, Vol. 10 (Spring 1959): 57–58.

66–67: **Schooners at Boston's T Wharf, 1880s**
MAIN IMAGE:
a. Baldwin Coolidge (1845–1928), photographer.
ADDITIONAL IMAGES:
b. Advertisement for ship caboose stoves manufactured and sold by F. D. Chase, Boston, from *Gaylor's Shipbuilders and Outfitters Directory of the Seaboard Cities of the United States.* (New York: Gaylor & Whitmore, 1875.) Courtesy Capt. W. J. L. Parker, USCG (ret.).
c. Postcard of T Wharf and Fish District, Boston, 1911 or earlier. Publisher unknown.
d. Advertisement for John R. Neal & Co.,

Boston, from September 14, 1901 issue of *The Fishing Gazette.* Courtesy W. H. Bunting.
PRINCIPAL RESOURCES:
Bunting, W. H., compiler and editor. *A Day's Work: A Sampler of Historic Maine Photographs, 1860–1920.* Gardiner, Maine: Tilbury House; Portland, Maine: Maine Preservation, 2000: 168.

68–69: **Landing a Halibut, T Wharf, Boston, c. 1885**
MAIN IMAGE:
Baldwin Coolidge (1845–1928), photographer
PRINCIPAL RESOURCES:
Goode, George B. *The Fisheries and Fishery Industries of the United States.* Washington: Government Printing Office, 1884–1887: Sec. V, 3–89.

70–71: **Atlantic Avenue, Boston, November, 1900**
MAIN IMAGE:
a.1.–a.4. Possibly for the Boston Elevated Railway, possibly Paul Rowell (active 1898–1935), photographer.
PRINCIPAL RESOURCES:
Whitehill, Walter Muir. *Boston: A Topographical History.* Cambridge, Massachusetts: Harvard University Press, 1968: 219–20.

72–73: **T Wharf, Boston, January 9, 1902**
MAIN IMAGE:
Nathaniel L. Stebbins (1847–1922), photographer.
PRINCIPAL RESOURCES:
Fishermen of the Atlantic. Boston: Fishing Masters' Association, Inc., 1909: 85.

74–75: *Servia* / **Immigration Quarters, East Boston, December 28, 1910**
MAIN IMAGES:
a.1. Nathaniel L. Stebbins (1847–1922), photographer.
a.2. The Boston and Albany Railroad Company, photographer.
ADDITIONAL IMAGES:
b. Postcard of the Cunard R.M.S. *Ivernia* and *Saxonia,* 1919 or earlier. Publisher unknown.
c. Cover photograph, *From Immigrant Ship to Citizenship,* from the North Bennet Street Industrial School's *Bulletin, 1921–1922.*
PRINCIPAL RESOURCES:
Twenty-Second Annual Report of the Boston Chamber of Commerce. Boston: Chamber of Commerce, 1908: 42.

76–77: **Fire, East Boston, August 26, 1907**
MAIN IMAGE:
a. The Boston and Albany Railroad Company, photographer.

ADDITIONAL IMAGES:
b. Cover of the *Souvenir View Book of the Chelsea Ruins.* (The Metropolitan News Co., c. 1908.)
Background. Postcard of Fireboat in Action, Boston, c. 1906. Detroit Publishing Co., publisher.

78–79: *City of Bangor*, **Boston, 5 p.m., August 12, 1906** / *City of Bangor*, **Sunk, Federal Wharf, East Boston, April 19, 1934**
MAIN IMAGES:
a.1. Nathaniel L. Stebbins (1847–1922), photographer.
a.2. R. L. Graham (active 1930s–1960s), photographer. Courtesy The Steamship Historical Society of America, Providence, Rhode Island.
ADDITIONAL IMAGES:
b. Pass for the Portland Steamship Co., 1901.
c. Pass for the Casco Bay Steamboat Co., 1902.
d. Postcard of the steamer "City of Bangor" at Hampden Narrows, Penobscot River, Bangor, Maine, 1907 or earlier. The Metropolitan News Co., publisher.
e. Pass for the Casco Bay Steamboat Co., 1899.
PRINCIPAL RESOURCES:
Richardson, John M. *Steamboat Lore of the Penobscot: An Informal Story of Steamboating in Maine's Penobscot Region.* Augusta, Maine: Kennebec Journal Print Shop, 1941: 19.

80–81: **The Boston-East Boston Ferry** *Noddle Island*, **November 2, 1911** / **Tug** *Saturn*, **Boston, November 27, 1911**
MAIN IMAGES:
a.1. Photographer unknown.
a.2. Nathaniel L. Stebbins (1847–1922), photographer.
ADDITIONAL IMAGES:
b. Panoramic postcard of Boston Harbor and Waterfront, c. 1906. Detroit Publishing Co., publisher. Courtesy W. H. Bunting.
c. Pass for the East Boston Ferry, 1844.
d. Foot-Pass for the East Boston Ferry.
e. Advertisement for the Boston Tow-Boat Company from *Gaylor's Shipbuilders and Outfitters Directory of the Seaboard Cities of the United States.* (New York: Gaylor & Whitmore, 1875.) Courtesy Capt. W. J. L. Parker, USCG (ret.).
PRINCIPAL RESOURCES:
City Document No. 11, for 1894, Boston, Massachusetts: 9.

**82–83: The Deck of the *Gitana*, 1883 /
Gitana's Saloon or Main Cabin, 1884**
MAIN IMAGES:
a.1–a.2. Nathaniel L. Stebbins (1847–1922),
photographer.
ADDITIONAL IMAGES:
b. Postcard of Hull Harbor, Massachusetts,
1907 or earlier. The New England News
Company, publisher.
c. Trade catalogue cover for A. J. Wilkinson
& Co.'s Boat Builder's Hardware, Boston.
d. Advertisement for Howard Place Uni-
form Outfitter from *The Illustrated Coast
Pilot.* (Boston: N. L. Stebbins, 1896.)
PRINCIPAL RESOURCES:
Anderson, Isabel. *Under the Black Horse
Flag.* Boston and New York: Houghton
Mifflin, 1926.

**84–85: The Start of the City Regatta,
Boston Harbor, July 4, 1887**
MAIN IMAGE:
a. Nathaniel L. Stebbins (1847–1922),
photographer.
ADDITIONAL IMAGES:
b. "Flags of Yacht Clubs" from the Boston
Yacht Club's 1894 Constitution and Bylaws.
Courtesy W. H. Bunting.
c. Cover of the *Boston Yacht Club Yearbook*,
1911.

**86–87: U.S.S. *Wabash*, Boston Navy Yard,
Charlestown, Massachusetts, 1890s**
MAIN IMAGE:
a. Photographer unknown.
ADDITIONAL IMAGES:
b, c, d, f, g. Stereo views, "View from
Bridge of the Battleship Minnesota," "One
of the Close Shaves of a Sailor's Life," "The
Ship's Tailor," "A Liberty Party," and "The
Mascot of the Flagship Connecticut," from
the printed stereoscopic set, *Uncle Sam's
Fighting Ships*, c. 1900. Publisher unknown.
e. Photograph of the U.S.S. *Wabash*. Mary
H. Northend (1850–1926), photographer.
PRINCIPAL RESOURCES:
Bunting, W. H., compiler and annotator.
Portrait of a Port: Boston, 1852–1914.
Cambridge, Massachusetts: Harvard
University Press, 1971: 438.
King, Stanton H. *Dog-Watches at Sea.*
Boston: Houghton Mifflin, 1901.
Morison, Samuel Eliot. *One Boy's Boston,
1887–1901.* Boston: Houghton Mifflin,
1962: 54.

88–89: *Missouri*, October 21, 1903
MAIN IMAGE:
a. Nathaniel L. Stebbins (1847–1922),
photographer.
ADDITIONAL IMAGES:
b. Chromolithograph of the U. S. Battleship
Iowa, 1898. Koerner & Hayes, publisher.
c. Page from a promotional calendar issued
by The Strobridge Litho. Co., Cincinnati,
Ohio, 1905.
d. Recruitment card for the U.S. Navy.
PRINCIPAL RESOURCES:
Boston Evening Transcript, October 22, 1903.

**90–91: Brant Rock Beach, Marshfield,
Massachusetts, mid-1890s**
MAIN IMAGE:
a. L. B. Howard (active early 1890s),
photographer.
ADDITIONAL IMAGES:
b. Panoramic postcard of Brant Rock,
Massachusetts. Publisher unknown.
c. Postcard of Fourth of July firecrackers.
International Art Publishing Co., publisher.
d. Postcard of children celebrating the
Fourth of July. Publisher unknown.
e. Pamphlet, "South Shore of Massachusetts Bay." (A. B. Smith, publisher, for the
New York, New Haven and Hartford Railroad Co., 1910.)
PRINCIPAL RESOURCES:
Krusell, Cynthia Hagar, and Betty Magoun
Bates. *Marshfield, A Town of Villages,
1640–1990.* Marshfield Hills, Massachusetts: Historical Research Associates,
1990.

**92–93: Life-Savers, Orleans, Massachu-
setts, February 25, 1899 / *Frances*, Truro,
Massachusetts, 1873**
MAIN IMAGES:
a.1. Photographer unknown.
a.2. George H. Nickerson (1835–1890),
photographer.
ADDITIONAL IMAGES:
b. Engraving, "Rescued from the Wreck,"
from *Cast Away in the Cold: An Old Man's
Story of a Young Man's Adventures, as Related by Captain John Hardy, Mariner* by Dr.
Isaac I. Hayes. (Boston: Lee and Sheppard,
Publishers, 1888.) Private Collection.
c. Periodical cover for the July 1925 issue
of *The Mentor*. Springfield, Ohio: The
Cromwell Publishing Company, publisher.
Private Collection.
d. Book cover of *Cast Away in the Cold:
An Old Man's Story of a Young Man's Ad-
ventures, as Related by Captain John Hardy,
Mariner* by Dr. Isaac I. Hayes. (Boston: Lee
and Sheppard, Publishers, 1888.) Private
Collection.
e. Book cover of *Darry the Life Saver* by
Frank V. Webster. (New York: Cupples &
Leon Company, 1911.) Private Collection.
f. Engraving, "Sitting, Stitching in a Mourn-
ful Muse," from the July 1874 issue of
Harper's New Monthly Magazine.
PRINCIPAL RESOURCES:
Shanks, Ralph, and Wick York. *The U.S.
Life-Saving Service: Heroes, Rescues, and
Architecture of the Early Coast Guard.* Lisa
Woo Shanks, editor. Petaluma, California:
Costaño Books, 1996: 8–11.
Small, Isaac M. *Shipwrecks on Cape Cod.* Old
Greenwich, Connecticut: Chatham Press,
1970: 14–20.

**94–95: Porch-Sitting, the Chequesset
Inn, Wellfleet, Massachusetts, 1913**
MAIN IMAGE:
a. The New England News Company (active
c. 1905–1925), photographer.
ADDITIONAL IMAGES:
b. Postcard of the New Ocean Hotel,
Swampscott, Massachusetts, c. 1908. The
Hugh C. Leighton Co., publisher.
c. Postcard of the Chequesset Inn, Well-
fleet, Massachusetts, 1907 or earlier. Sou-
venir Post Card Co., publisher.
d. Postcard of Girl and B(u)oy on the Maine
Coast, c. 1909. The Hugh C. Leighton Co.,
publisher. Courtesy Maine Historic Preservation Commission.
e. Postcard of the Colonial, Watch Hill,
Rhode Island, 1915 or earlier. The Rhode
Island News Company, publisher.
PRINCIPAL RESOURCES:
[Bangor] *Industrial Journal*, January 19, 1894.
With thanks to: Captain Reuben Baker.

96–97: Postcard of the Nantasket House
at Night, Nantasket Beach, Massachusetts.
United Art Co., publisher.

**98–99: Codfish Curing, Provincetown,
Massachusetts, 1870s**
MAIN IMAGE:
a. George H. Nickerson (1835–1890) and
William M. Smith (active 1870s–1880s),
photographers.
ADDITIONAL IMAGES:
b. Postcard of Provincetown Harbor from
Town Hill, Provincetown, Massachusetts,
1907 or earlier. Souvenir Post Card Co.,
publisher.
c. Trade card for Henry Mayo & Co. minced
codfish, Boston.
d. Postcard of Fishermen, Provincetown,
Massachusetts, 1922 or earlier. The Metropolitan News Co., publisher.
PRINCIPAL RESOURCES:
Goode, George B. *The Fisheries and Fishery
Industries of the United States.* Washington: Government Printing Office.
1884–1887: Sec. II, 127, 226.
Thoreau, Henry David. *Cape Cod.* New York:
Norton, 1951: 14.

100–101: Blackfish, Probably on the Bay Side of Cape Cod, c. 1900
MAIN IMAGE:
Photographer unknown.
PRINCIPAL RESOURCES:
Tarbell, Arthur Wilson. *Cape Cod Ahoy! A Travel Book for the Summer Visitor.* Boston: A. T. Ramsay, 1932: 52, 182.
Thoreau, Henry David. *Cape Cod.* New York: Norton, 1951: 14.

102–103: Old Windmill, West Falmouth, Massachusetts, c. 1890
MAIN IMAGE:
a. Baldwin Coolidge (1845–1928), photographer.
ADDITIONAL IMAGES:
b. Postcard of Old Wind Mill, Falmouth, Massachusetts, 1911 or earlier. Valentine & Sons' Pub. Co., Ltd., publisher.
c. Matchbook cover advertising Dutchland Farms Ice Cream, Brockton, Massachusetts.
PRINCIPAL RESOURCES:
Thoreau, Henry David. *Cape Cod.* New York: Norton, 1951: 14.
Witzell, Susan Fletcher, Jane A. McLaughlin, and Mary Lou Smith. *New England Views: The Photography of Baldwin Coolidge (1845–1928).* Woods Hole, Massachusetts: Woods Hole Historical Collections, 1998: 2.

104–105: Falmouth Heights, Massachusetts, c. 1910
MAIN IMAGES:
a.1–a.2. The New England News Company (active c. 1905–1925)
ADDITIONAL IMAGES:
b. Illustrations of base ball batting attitudes from *George Wright's Book For 1875, Containing Record of the Boston Base Ball Club.* (*The Norfolk County Gazette,* publisher, 1875.)
c, e, f. Illustrations for Wright and Ditson Sporting Goods 1928 Spring and Summer catalogue.
d. Postcard of Ball Game, Falmouth Heights, Massachusetts. Tichnor Brothers, publisher.
PRINCIPAL RESOURCES:
Price, Christopher. *Baseball by the Beach: History of America's National Pastime on Cape Cod.* Hyannis, Massachusetts: Parnassus Imprints, 1998: 176.
Tarbell, Arthur Wilson. *Cape Cod Ahoy! A Travel Book for the Summer Visitor.* Boston: A. T. Ramsay, 1932: 338–56.

106–107: *Augustus Hunt*, Boston, late 1880s
MAIN IMAGE:
Baldwin Coolidge (1845–1928), photographer.

PRINCIPAL RESOURCES:
United States Department of the Treasury, Bureau of Navigation. *Report of the Commissioner of Navigation to the Secretary of the Treasury.* Washington: Government Printing Office, 1887: 331.

108–109: Lightship in Ice, January 22, 1893
MAIN IMAGE:
a. Nathaniel L. Stebbins (1847–1922), photographer.
ADDITIONAL IMAGES:
b. Photograph of the lightship *Handkerchief No. 4.* Photographer unknown.
c. Postcard of the Wreck of the *Juniata* at Cohasset, Massachusetts, c. 1905. The New England News Company, publisher.
d. Cover of *Pictorial Chronicles of the Mighty Deep, Or The Sea, Its Ships & Sailors.* Francis Watt, editor. (London: James Sangster & Company, late nineteenth century.) Private Collection.
e. Postcard of the Hotel Nantasket with ice 25 feet high, c. 1905. The New England News Company, publisher.
PRINCIPAL RESOURCES:
Willoughby, Malcolm F. *Lighthouses of New England.* Boston: Metcalf, 1920: 178–95.

110–111: *Tecumseh*, April 1, 1890
MAIN IMAGE:
a. Nathaniel L. Stebbins (1847–1922), photographer.
ADDITIONAL IMAGES:
b. Poster advertising the Works of the New England Gas and Coke Company, Everett, Massachusetts. George H. Walker & Co., lithographer.
c. Photograph of a coal elevator and the barge *General McClellan,* Grand Junction Yard, East Boston. The Boston and Albany Railroad Company, photographer.
d. Advertisement for Rawson & Hittinger Hoisting Engines, Cambridgeport, Massachusetts, from *Gaylor's Shipbuilders and Outfitters Directory of the Seaboard Cities of the United States.* (New York: Gaylor & Whitmore, publisher, 1875.) Courtesy Capt. W. J. L. Parker, USCG (ret.).
PRINCIPAL RESOURCES:
Parker, W. J. Lewis. *The Great Coal Schooners of New England, 1870–1909.* Mystic, Connecticut: Marine Historical Association, 1948.

112–113: Siasconset Village, Nantucket, Massachusetts, 1880s
MAIN IMAGES:
a.1. Baldwin Coolidge (1845–1928), photographer.

a.2. Henry Sherman Wyer (1847–1920), photographer.
ADDITIONAL IMAGES:
Background. Postcard of Castle Bandbox, Siasconset Village, Nantucket Island, Massachusetts. H. Marshall Gardiner, publisher. Courtesy Geraldine Gardiner Salisbury.
PRINCIPAL RESOURCES:
Karttunen, Frances Ruley. *The Other Islanders: People Who Pulled Nantucket's Oars.* New Bedford, Massachusetts: Spinner Publications, 2005: 243–67.
Lancaster, Clay. *Nantucket in the Nineteenth Century.* New York: Dover, 1979: 95–103.

114–115: Siasconset Village, Nantucket, Massachusetts, 1880s
MAIN IMAGE:
Henry Sherman Wyer (1847–1920), photographer.

116–117: The Wreck of the *Wm. F. Marshall*, March 9, 1877
MAIN IMAGE:
a. Josiah Freeman (1834–1902), photographer.
ADDITIONAL IMAGES:
b. Trade card for Ayer's Hair Vigor. Dr. J. C. Ayer & Co., publisher.
c. Postcard of the Breeches Buoy in Action c. 1909. IPCN & Co., publisher.
PRINCIPAL RESOURCES:
Wrecks Around Nantucket. Compiled by Arthur H. Gardner. New Bedford, Massachusetts, 1915: 89.

118–119: Thomas Sandsbury, Tuckernuck Island, Massachusetts, c. 1884
MAIN IMAGE:
a. William Sturgis Bigelow (1850–1926), photographer.
ADDITIONAL IMAGES:
b. Photograph of William Sturgis Bigelow and an unidentified man on porch at Tuckernuck, Tuckernuck Island, Massachusetts. Courtesy Edward Wayman Coffin.
c. Photograph of Dr. Bigelow's place, Tuckernuck Island, Massachusetts. Photographer unknown.
d. Cover of *Japanese Homes and Their Surroundings* by Edward S. Morse. (New York: Harper & Brothers, 1895.) Private Collection.
e. Trade card for S.Y. Tank Co. Fancy Goods, Boston, c. 1900.
f. Postcard for Rich's Grill, Boston, c. 1907.
PRINCIPAL RESOURCES:
Coffin, Edward Wayman. *Tuckernuck Island: A Pictorial Review of the Island with Facts and Misinformation for the Uninformed.* Rockland, Massachusetts: Privately printed, 2000: 43.

Coffin, Edward Wayman. *Nantucket's Forgotten Island, Muskeget: As Viewed and Compiled on an Ebb Tide.* Rockland, Massachusetts: Privately printed, 1996.

120–121: Oak Bluffs, Martha's Vineyard, Massachusetts, 1905 or later

MAIN IMAGE:
a. Thomson and Thomson (active c. 1905–1915), photographers.

ADDITIONAL IMAGES:
b. Souvenir postcard book of Oak Bluffs, Massachusetts. Publisher unknown.
c. Stereo view of Clinton Ave. from Spinney's Camp Ground, Martha's Vineyard, Massachusetts, 1875. C. H. Shute & Son, photographers.
d. Stereo view of beach scene, Martha's Vineyard, Massachusetts. Photographer unknown.
e. Postcard of women bathers. Publisher unknown.
f. Postcard of the steamer *Uncatena*, Oak Bluffs, Massachusetts. J. N. Chamberlain, publisher.

PRINCIPAL RESOURCES:
Hough, Henry Beetle. *Martha's Vineyard, Summer Resort, After 100 Years.* Edgartown, Massachusetts: Avery's, 1966: 63–83.

122–123: Gay Head Light, Martha's Vineyard, Massachusetts, 1887 / The Cedars of West Chop, Martha's Vineyard, Massachusetts, 1891

MAIN IMAGES:
a.1–a.2. Baldwin Coolidge (1845–1928), photographer.

ADDITIONAL IMAGES:
b. Postcard of the steamer *Gay Head*, c. 1909. The Metropolitan News Co., publisher.
c. Photograph of whaleboat and rescuers, Gay Head, Martha's Vineyard, Massachusetts, 1884. Baldwin Coolidge, photographer.

PRINCIPAL RESOURCES:
Hough, George A. *Disaster on Devil's Bridge.* Mystic, Connecticut: Marine Historical Association, 1963: 68–73.
Hough, Henry Beetle. *Martha's Vineyard, Summer Resort, After 100 Years.* Edgartown, Massachusetts: Avery's, 1966: 102, 230.

124–125: Gay Head, Martha's Vineyard, Massachusetts, 1894

MAIN IMAGE:
a. Baldwin Coolidge (1845–1928), photographer.

ADDITIONAL IMAGES:
b. Postcard of Gay Head Cliffs, Martha's Vineyard, Massachusetts. Thomson & Thomson, publishers.

PRINCIPAL RESOURCES:
Willoughby, Malcolm F. *Lighthouses of New England.* Boston: Metcalf, 1920: 197–202.

126–127: Captain and Mrs. Obed Delano, Marion, Massachusetts, c. 1890

MAIN IMAGE:
a. Photographer unknown.

ADDITIONAL IMAGES:
b. Detail of main image.
c. Postcard of Sperm Whaling, "The Capture," New Bedford, Massachusetts, 1916 or earlier H. S. Hutchinson & Co., publisher.
d. Sheet music cover for "The Mariner's Orphan Girl." Words by Thomas S. Hodson and music by N. J. Sporle. E. W. Bouvé, lithographer. Oliver Ditson, publisher.
e. Daguerreotype of a gold mining scene. Photographer unknown.

PRINCIPAL RESOURCES:
Somers, Olive Hiller. *Old Landing Days in Marion.* Marion, Massachusetts: [n.p.] 1965: 55.
Somers, Olive Hiller. *Three Centuries of Marion Houses.* Marion, Massachusetts: Sippican Historical Society, 1972.

128–129: Merrill's Wharf, New Bedford, Massachusetts, c. 1870

MAIN IMAGE:
a. Photographer unknown.

ADDITIONAL IMAGES:
b. Postcard of Speeders, Holmes Mill, New Bedford, Massachusetts, 1916 or earlier. H.S. Hutchinson & Co., publisher.
c. Cloth label for Cocheco Mills, as sold by Lawrence and Co., Boston, c. 1866.
d. Postcard of Casks of Whale Oil awaiting a market, New Bedford, Massachusetts, 1907 or earlier. The Rotograph Co., publisher.

130–131: *Reliance*, July 25, 1903

MAIN IMAGE:
a. Nathaniel L. Stebbins (1847–1922), photographer.

ADDITIONAL IMAGES:
b. Ticket to the launching of the cup defender *Reliance*, April 11, 1903. Courtesy The Herreshoff Marine Museum/America's Cup Hall of Fame, Bristol, Rhode Island.

c. Photograph of the *Reliance*, 1903. James Burton, photographer. Courtesy Mystic Seaport, Rosenfeld Collection, Mystic, Connecticut. Image #B655.1.
d. Book cover of *The America's Cup Races* by Herbert L. Stone. (New York: The Macmillan Company, 1930.)

PRINCIPAL RESOURCES:
Herreshoff, L. Francis. *An Introduction to Yachting.* New York: Sheridan House, 1963: 150–51.

132–133: *Olive E*, August 9, 1906

MAIN IMAGE:
a. Nathaniel L. Stebbins (1847–1922), photographer.

ADDITIONAL IMAGES:
Background. Page from the promotional publication, *50 Fish from American Waters.* Allen & Ginter, Manufacturers of Cigarettes, publisher. Private Collection.

134–135: Mystic, Connecticut, 1890s

MAIN IMAGE:
a. Photographer unknown.

ADDITIONAL IMAGES:
b. Postcard of Harbor, Bridgeport, Connecticut, c. 1905. H.C. Leighton Co., publisher.
c. Postcard of the schooner *Elvira Ball* of Mystic, Connecticut. H. D. Utley, publisher.

PRINCIPAL RESOURCES:
With thanks to: William Peterson, Senior Curator, Mystic Seaport, and Paul Stubing.

136–137: *Priscilla* Interior, 1920s (?) / *Priscilla*, August 21, 1896

MAIN IMAGES:
a.1. William King Covell (1904–1975), photographer.
a.2. Nathaniel L. Stebbins (1847–1922), photographer.

ADDITIONAL IMAGES:
b. Programme of Concerts for the steamer *Providence*, February, 1890.
c. Illustration of a steamship engine room. Artist unknown.
d. Postcard for the Fall River Line of The New England Steamship Company.

PRINCIPAL RESOURCES:
McAdam, Roger Williams. *The Old Fall River Line.* New York: Stephen Daye Press, 1955.